Popular Mechanics

THE GIRL MECHANIC

Popular Mechanics

THE GIRL
MECHANIC

CLASSIC CRAFTS, GAMES,
and TOYS *to* BUILD

HEARST BOOKS
A division of Sterling Publishing Co., Inc.

New York / London
www.sterlingpublishing.com

Design by Barbara Balch

Library of Congress Cataloging-in-Publication Data
Popular mechanics : the girl mechanic : classic crafts, games, and toys to build / The editors of Popular mechanics.
    p. cm.
  Includes index.
  ISBN 978-1-58816-610-4
  1. Handicraft—Juvenile literature. 2. Handicraft for girls—Juvenile literature. I. Popular mechanics (Chicago, Ill. : 1959) II. Title: Girl mechanic.
  TT160.P69 2009
  745.5—dc22

                                    2008026089

10 9 8 7 6 5 4 3 2 1

Published by Hearst Books
A division of Sterling Publishing Co., Inc.
387 Park Avenue South, New York, NY 10016

Popular Mechanics and Hearst Books are trademarks of
Hearst Communications, Inc.

www.popularmechanics.com

For information about custom editions, special sales, premium and corporate purchases, please contact Sterling Special Sales Department at 800-805-5489 or specialsales@sterlingpublishing.com.

Distributed in Canada by Sterling Publishing
c/o Canadian Manda Group, 165 Dufferin Street
Toronto, Ontario, Canada M6K 3H6

Distributed in Australia by Capricorn Link (Australia) Pty. Ltd.
P.O. Box 704, Windsor, NSW 2756 Australia

Manufactured in China

Sterling ISBN 978-1-58816-610-4

CONTENTS

FOREWORD

In these days of MySpace and text messaging, it seems harder than ever for parents to find quality time with their daughter. But no longer! What a family needs is a good project that everyone can sink their teeth into and enjoy, something that is not only interesting and pleasurable as a pursuit, but that also yields a worthwhile result. That's where *The Girl Mechanic* comes in.

Simply put, this book is full of projects that will bring families closer together, all in the name of fun and creativity.

Like its predecessors, *The Boy Mechanic* and *The Boy Mechanic Makes Toys*, the projects offered by *The Girl Mechanic* are exercises in creativity *and* help develop useful skills. From the eight-year-old who's helping sand the corners off a home-built backyard slide, to the 10-year-old who's designing her own Christmas cards, to the teenager doing most of the construction for a pull toy for her toddler brother, any girl is sure to gain essential knowledge and abilities that will serve her going forward in life.

Of course, the finished projects themselves represent their own reward. The enterprising girl can create a whole range of gifts for Mom and Dad, from delicate and elegant picture frames to one-of-kind hand-worked copper bowls. There are also gifts for the younger children in the family including toys and furniture that will fill a function while serving to amuse. Some of the projects provide wonderful games that will bring a whole new dimension to family fun, including basement miniature golf courses, and tabletop miniature bowling. The delights are nearly unlimited.

Beyond such amusements, many opportunities exist between these covers for any girl to exercise the artist within. Whether she's creating fascinating abstract pattern drawings with a homemade "wondergraph," or weaving beautiful objects on a loom that she helped construct, *The Girl Mechanic* is often *The Girl Artist*.

And there's so much more. From sporting instruction and devices to keep a girl in health and fitness, to the ever-popular dollhouses—there's even one with an elevator—*The Girl Mechanic* provides the perfect chance for families to unite in fun and make memories they'll cherish forever.

The Editors
of *Popular Mechanics*

{ CHAPTER 1 }

CRAFTY FUN

—

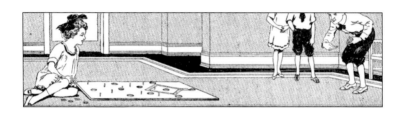

THE ART *of the* RAINY DAY

— WEAVING RAGS INTO RUGS —

There's a lot of fun in weaving rags into colorful serviceable rugs, and it's a craft that girls and their parents can enjoy together.

HOOKED RUGS: Here you need a wooden frame—an old window screen will do—and a suitable weaving hook. Details *A, B,* and *C* in *Fig. 1* show three ways of assembling a frame. The peg arrangement permits adjustment to take rugs of different sizes, while the clamping method makes it easy to take up slack as the

work progresses. Detail *E* shows how to proportion the frame to the pattern, and *D* shows a method for laying out an oval. The frame is covered with burlap or coarse linen and is either fastened with thumbtacks or stitched to cloth sleeves, as in *B.* Keep the threads of the burlap running parallel with the frame and allow sufficient material to turn under and hem later. A rug hook is made by shortening the shank of an ice pick and filing a hook like that shown in *Fig. 1,* detail *F.*

Suggestions for appropriate patterns can be found by thumbing through design or craftwork magazines. Enlarge the chosen pattern to full size and draw it on the burlap with a crayon. Then, working outward from the center, push the hook through the burlap, *G.* Pull a strip of ½-in. cloth up through to form a

loop ½ in. long, *H.* Push the hook through again, three strands from the first insertion, and draw up another loop, *I.* When a row has been completed, the loops can be clipped, *J,* or they may be left uncut. From here on it is simply a matter of repeating as before. Certain portions of the design can be made to stand out in relief by allowing the loops to extend higher than the others.

FLUFF RUGS: Although similar to a hooked rug, the fluff rug is a continuous strip of material wound in a spiral and sewed together, as in *D, Fig. 3,* to form a thick, soft rug. First, wind a ¾-in. strip of cloth around a

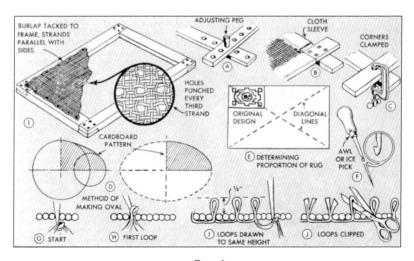

FIG. 1

FIG. 2

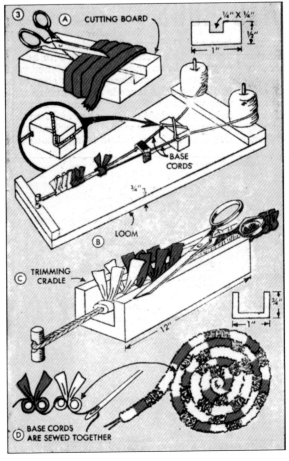

FIG. 3

grooved board and cut, as in *A*. Then with a loom made and rigged with a carpet warp, as in *B*, begin attaching the cloth strips to the warp. These are not tied but simply brought up between the cords, as at *D*, and pushed together as you go. When the length has been built out to a foot or so, place a trimming board under the cord and snip the tops off evenly. Proceed as before until you have a length of "fluff" sufficient to complete the size rug desired. Strips of white, yellow, and black will give a pleasing mottled effect.

WOVEN RUGS: For these you'll need a loom such as the one in *A, Fig. 4*, on which you can turn out throw rugs up to 16 by 24 in. The loom is rigged with regular carpet warp by running it back and forth and around the nail heads at the ends. Two heddles—one being notched—are used alternately to raise the warp strands, as in *D* and *E*. First, the plain heddle is set edgewise to raise one set of warps, then the shuttle is passed through, after which the heddle is placed flat. The same is done with the notched heddle that produces a pattern, as in *C*. After each passing of

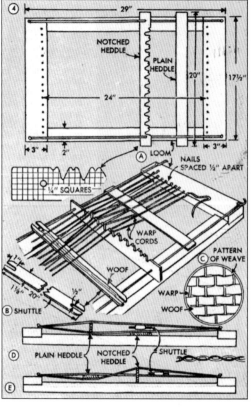

FIG. 4

the shuttle, the woof is crowded against the previous strand. Sample designs *A* to *G*, inclusively, in *Fig. 2*, can be enlarged to full size by ruling an equal number of larger squares on paper and transferring the design to each respective square.

— WEAVING BLOCKS —

Weaving blocks will keep the youngsters entertained for hours. Dowel pegs fitted in wooden bases provide forms on which string is wound in and out around the pegs like a basket. When finished, stiffen the woven work with shellac before removing it from the base.

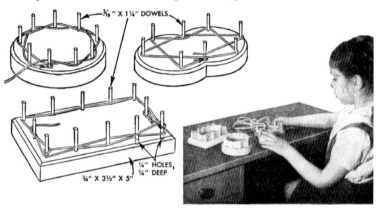

— TRY YOUR HAND

AT GIMP BRAIDING —

Few crafts require so little equipment as gimp braiding. In addition to the gimp, about all that is needed is a pointed stick. The steps for braiding belts and bracelets are given here, but with a little practice, you can braid many other attractive and useful articles.

Materials: Gimp consists of cotton tape covered with tough, flexible lacquer and is available by the yard, or in 50- and 100-yard spools in various colors. Standard widths are 3/32 and ⅛ in., although wider gimp can be obtained. Plastic gimp is also available. Most of the projects pictured in this article were braided from ⅛-in. flat gimp.

FLAT BRAID

(12-STRAND): To make a belt braided with 12 strands, use six pieces of gimp 3 yds. long and loop them through a suitable buckle as shown in *Fig. 2*. The buckle is lipped over nails driven into a block of wood that is clamped to a table as shown at right. Start braiding by turning the left-hand strand over itself, *Fig. 3*. Then braid the remain-

ing strands as in *Fig. 4*. This is the completed starting position. Now, tighten the braid and then start the running braid. This is done by taking the top right-hand strand and weaving it over and under the others as shown in *Fig. 5*. Repeat the procedure with the top left-hand strand and braid right- and left-hand strands

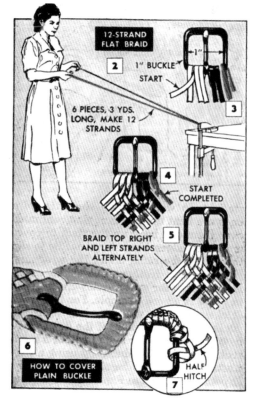

12-STRAND FLAT BRAID

2 1″ BUCKLE START

3

6 PIECES, 3 YDS. LONG, MAKE 12 STRANDS

4

START COMPLETED

5 BRAID TOP RIGHT AND LEFT STRANDS ALTERNATELY

6 HOW TO COVER PLAIN BUCKLE

7 HALF HITCH

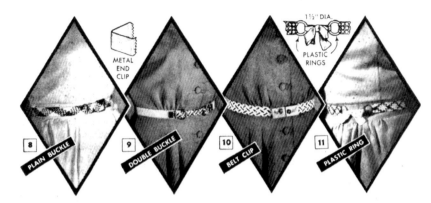

8 PLAIN BUCKLE

METAL END CLIP

9 DOUBLE BUCKLE

10 BELT CLIP

1½" DIA.

PLASTIC RINGS

11 PLASTIC RING

alternately in this way until the belt reaches the desired length. To finish the braid, as seen in *Fig. 12,* tuck the two outer strands, shown by loops, back under the braid for about two stitches. Unbraid the two middle strands (red and black) and turn them under and through the loops as in *Fig. 13.* Then braid the even-numbered strands back over the top for a distance of one or two stitches, as in *Fig. 14,* and cut off the excess gimp. Braid the remaining strands in the same way, but turn them under.

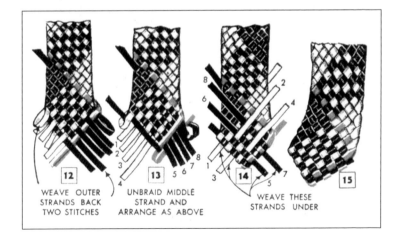

12 WEAVE OUTER STRANDS BACK TWO STITCHES

13 UNBRAID MIDDLE STRAND AND ARRANGE AS ABOVE

14 WEAVE THESE STRANDS UNDER

15

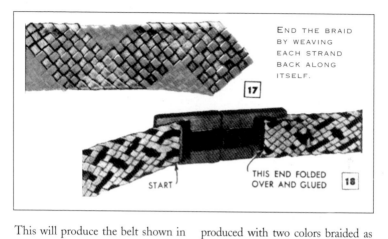

 END THE BRAID
BY WEAVING
EACH STRAND
BACK ALONG
ITSELF.

17

THIS END FOLDED
OVER AND GLUED **18**

START

This will produce the belt shown in *Figs. 15* and *17*.

BELT STYLES:
Many different kinds of belts can be made with 12-strand flat braiding. The pattern itself has numerous variations and depends upon arrangement of strands at the beginning. The strongest pattern is

produced with two colors braided as in *Fig. 19*. Popular variations are

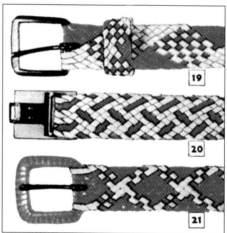

19

20

21

22

DROPPING A STRAND

BELT PATTERNS DEPEND ON HOW STRANDS
ARE ARRANGED AT START. HERE ARE
THREE VARIATIONS.

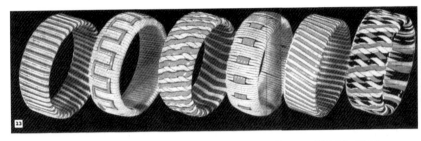

BRACELET STYLES: FROM LEFT, WRAP-AROUND, BASKET WEAVE, FLAT BRAID, BASKET WEAVE, WRAP-AROUND (DIAGONAL), FLAT BRAID

shown in *Figs. 20* and *21*. Belts are most effective when the pattern is simple and of not more than three colors. One-color belts are very attractive. *Fig. 8* shows a conventional buckle style. In *Fig. 9*, the belt has a buckle at both ends, the second buckle being fastened by folding the braid over and cementing or sewing it. The two buckles are spanned by a short length of flat braid, the ends of which are finished with metal clips. The belts in *Figs. 1* and *10* are fitted with a belt clip set. The method of attaching the clips is shown in *Figs. 18* and *20*. The

belt in *Fig. 11* is braided and glued around plastic rings and is fastened with a tie ribbon. A 12-strand flat braid of ⅛-in. gimp will produce a belt 1 in. wide. If you want a narrower belt, do the braiding exactly

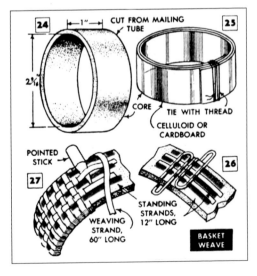

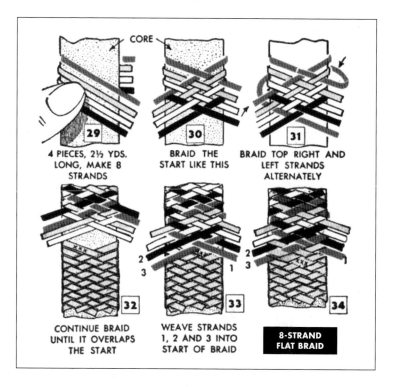

CORE

29 4 PIECES, 2½ YDS. LONG, MAKE 8 STRANDS

30 BRAID THE START LIKE THIS

31 BRAID TOP RIGHT AND LEFT STRANDS ALTERNATELY

32 CONTINUE BRAID UNTIL IT OVERLAPS THE START

33 WEAVE STRANDS 1, 2 AND 3 INTO START OF BRAID

34 8-STRAND FLAT BRAID

the same but use 8 or 10 strands instead of 12. If the end is to be folded over a buckle, it is best to drop one strand, as shown in *Fig. 22*. Plain buckles are much more attractive if covered with gimp, as in *Fig. 6*. To do this, the gimp is applied by the half-hitch method as in *Fig. 7*.

BRACELETS: Various styles of bracelets are shown in *Figs. 23* and 38. All are braided around a cardboard core. This can be cut from a mailing tube, *Fig. 24*, or made up from a strip of cardboard tied or held with gummed tape, as in *Fig. 25*. The wrap-around style, *Fig. 23*, detail *A*, is the simplest. It is made by wrapping two strands of different colors around the core, tucking the ends under. The wrapping can be straight across as in detail *A*, or diagonal, as in detail *E*.

BASKET WEAVE:
This popular style of
braiding is done with any
number of short standing
strands fastened to the
core with paper clips, as
shown in *Fig. 26,* after
which the single weaving
strand is carried round
and round and over and under to
make the pattern. The fastest
method of working is to pick up the
standing strands with a pointed
stick, *Fig. 27,* rather than lace the
weaving strand under. The basket-
weave pattern looks best when 3/32-
in. gimp is used, because it is thinner
than the ⅛-in. gimp and permits
closer weaving. Plastic gimp, being
tough and elastic, can be laced with a
needle after the entire core is covered
in a wrap-around manner. In either
case, the ending is made by weaving
the standing strands double, and
carrying the weaving strand to the
inside where it is tucked under or
glued.

FLAT BRAID (8-STRAND):
This takes more time than any other
kind of braiding, but is very effective,
especially with narrow gimp. Start
by looping four strands of gimp
through the bracelet core, as in

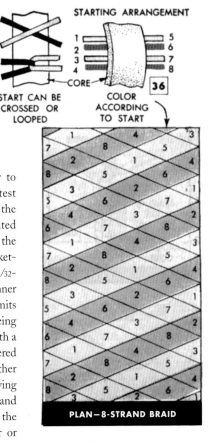

STARTING ARRANGEMENT

35 START CAN BE CROSSED OR LOOPED

36 COLOR ACCORDING TO START

CORE

PLAN—8-STRAND BRAID

Fig. 29. Braid the strands together,
Fig. 30, over the complete the starting end and tighten the braid. Then
proceed with the running braid. This
is done by passing the top right-
hand strand through the inside of
the core and out between the two

the diamonds to form the desired pattern. Then arrange the strands of gimp according to the numbers in the chart and the starting arrangement. Each number must always appear in the same color of diamond.

CROWN BRAID: This can be either square or round. Both use

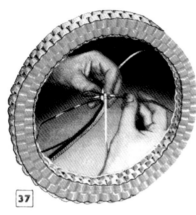

CROWN BRAID BRACELET

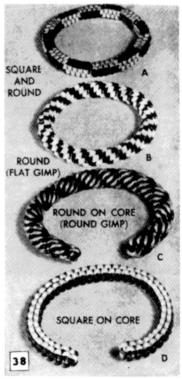

SQUARE
AND
ROUND

A

ROUND
(FLAT GIMP)

B

ROUND ON CORE
(ROUND GIMP)

C

SQUARE ON CORE

D

middle strands on the opposite side, *Fig. 31.* The left-hand top strand is worked in the same way and from then on the braid alternates right and left. *Fig. 32* shows the braid nearly completed. Continue until you completely cover the starting end, as in *Fig. 33,* and then weave strands 1, 2, and 3 into the beginning ends of the braid, *Fig. 34.* This brings all strands to the outside where they can be cut off or folded to the inside and glued. Numerous patterns can be made with 8-strand flat braid, the pattern depending on how the strands are arranged at the start. *Fig. 35* shows two starting methods and *Fig. 36* gives a pattern chart. Make a tracing of the chart and color

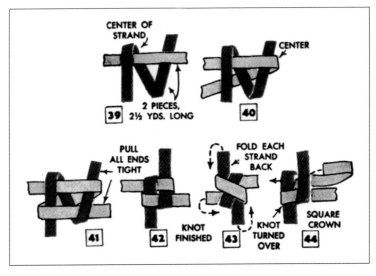

CENTER OF STRAND

39 2 PIECES, 2½ YDS. LONG

40 CENTER

PULL ALL ENDS TIGHT

41

42 KNOT FINISHED

FOLD EACH STRAND BACK

43 KNOT TURNED OVER

44 SQUARE CROWN

SAME STARTING KNOT IS USED FOR SQUARE OR ROUND CROWN.

the same starting knot, *Figs. 39* to *42*, inclusively. After making the knot, turn it over, as in *Fig. 43*, and begin braiding. The square crown is made by carrying each strand squarely across, as shown in *Fig. 44*. This produces the square, braided effect shown in *Fig. 37*. Although the round crown is done with flat braid, it results in a round, ropelike braid. At any stage of braiding the round crown, the top braid looks just like the square braid, *Fig. 47*. However, each succeeding layer is made by carrying the strands across

diagonally, as in *Figs. 48, 49,* and *50.* This braid is often called a spiral braid because it turns like a corkscrew, as can be seen in *Fig. 38*, details *B* and *C*. The color pattern can be changed by braiding several layers of square crown and then one layer of round crown, producing the effect shown in *Fig. 38*, detail *A*.

CLIP BRACELETS: These bracelets, *Fig. 38*, details *C* and *D*, fit snugly on the wrist and are popular for that reason. They can be made in either round or square crown, the braiding being done around a wire

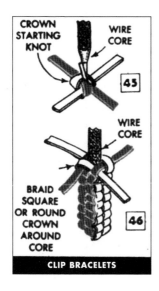

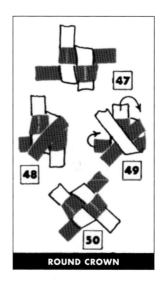

CLIP BRACELETS

ROUND CROWN

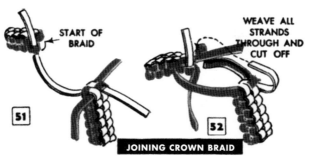

JOINING CROWN BRAID

core. Begin by hooking the wire into the starting knot, as shown in *Fig. 45,* and work the braid exactly as previously explained. *Fig. 46* shows the square crown. After the desired length is reached, the wire core is cut off and the braiding continued for two or three layers beyond the end of the wire, at which point the final layer is pulled tight

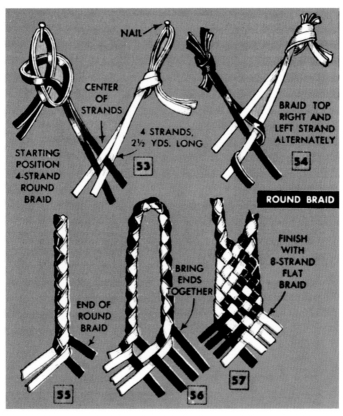

53 — STARTING POSITION 4-STRAND ROUND BRAID — NAIL — CENTER OF STRANDS — 4 STRANDS, 2½ YDS. LONG

54 — BRAID TOP RIGHT AND LEFT STRAND ALTERNATELY

ROUND BRAID

55 — END OF ROUND BRAID

56 — BRING ENDS TOGETHER

57 — FINISH WITH 8-STRAND FLAT BRAID

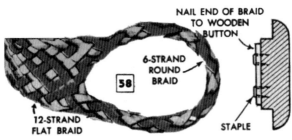

58 — NAIL END OF BRAID TO WOODEN BUTTON — 6-STRAND ROUND BRAID — 12-STRAND FLAT BRAID — STAPLE

and the ends woven back into the braiding.

JOINING CROWN BRAID: *Figs. 51* and *52* illustrate the joining of crown braid to make a complete ring or bracelet. This is done by weaving the strands back into the starting braid. This braid has a certain amount of stretch that permits slipping the bracelet over the hand.

ROUND BRAID: This braid is used mainly for leashes, but is shown worked into a loop-and-button belt. To do this, start by locating the center of four strands. Tie off one end and arrange the four strands, as shown in

Fig. 53. From this position, take the top right-hand strand and carry it under the braid and over between the two strands, *Fig. 54.* Do the same with the top left-hand strand and continue right and left alternately. The result is an attractive round braid, *Fig. 55.* Bring the two ends of the braid together and arrange the strands as shown in *Fig. 56.* You now have an 8-strand flat braid. Run this to the length desired, *Fig. 57,* then staple the end to a wooden button. The loop can be made with a 6-strand round braid, running into a 12-strand flat braid, as shown in *Fig. 58.*

— HOW TO MAKE A WONDERGRAPH —

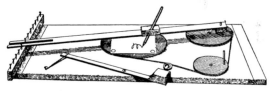

AN EASILY MADE WONDERGRAPH

The so-called wondergraph is an exceedingly interesting drawing machine, and the variety of designs it will produce—all symmetrical and ornamental, and some wonderfully complicated—is almost without limit. *Fig. 1* represents diagrammatically the machine shown in the sketch. This is the easiest to

make and gives as great a variety of results as any.

Three grooved circular disks are fastened with screws to a piece of wide board or a discarded box bottom, so that they revolve freely about their centers. They may be sawed from pieces of thin board. Use the largest one for the revolving table *T.*

G is the guide wheel and *D* the driver with attached handle. Secure a piece of a 36-in. ruler, which can be obtained from any furniture dealer, and nail a small block, about 1 in. thick, to one end. Drill a hole through both the ruler and the block, and pivot them by means of a wooden peg to the face of the guide wheel. A fountain pen, or a pencil, is placed at *P* and held securely by rubber bands in a grooved block attached to the ruler. A strip of wood, *MN*, is fastened to one end of the board. This strip is made just high enough to keep the ruler parallel with the surface of the table, and a row of small nails are driven partway into its upper edge. Any one of these nails may be used to hold the other end of the ruler in position, as shown in the sketch. If the wheels are not true, a belt tightener, *B*, may be attached and held against the belt with a spring or rubber band.

After the apparatus is adjusted so it will run smoothly, fasten a piece of drawing paper to the table with a couple of thumbtacks, adjust the pen so that it rests lightly on the paper, and turn the drive wheel. The results will be surprising and delightful. The accompanying designs were made with a very crude combination of

pulleys and belts, as described.

The machine should have a speed that will cause the pen to move over the paper at the same rate as in ordinary writing. The ink should flow freely from the pen as it passes over the paper. A very fine pen may be necessary to prevent the lines from running together.

The dimensions of the wondergraph may vary. The larger designs in the illustration were made on a table, 8 in. in diameter, which was driven by a guide wheel, 6 in. in diameter. The size of the driver has no effect on the form or dimensions of the design, but a change in almost any other part of the machine has a marked effect on the results obtained. Secure the penholder so that it may be fastened at various positions along the ruler, and drill holes through the guide wheel at different distances from the center to hold the peg attaching the ruler. These two adjustments, together with the one for changing the other end of the ruler by the rows of nails, will make a very great number of combinations possible. Even a slight change will greatly modify a figure or create an entirely new one. Designs may be changed by simply twisting the belt, thus reversing the direction of the table.

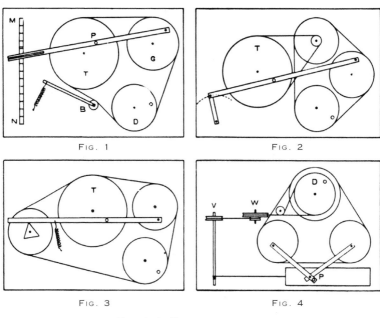

FIG. 1   FIG. 2

FIG. 3   FIG. 4

FIG. 1-4. DIAGRAMS SHOWING
CONSTRUCTION OF WONDERGRAPHS

If an arm is fastened to the ruler at right angles to it, containing three or four grooves to hold the pen, still different figures will be obtained. A novel effect is made by fastening two pens to this arm at the same time, one filled with red ink and the other with black ink. The designs will be quite dissimilar and may be one traced over the other or one within the other, according to the relative position of the pens.

Again change the size of the guide wheel and note the effect. If the diameter of the table is a multiple of that of the guide wheel, a complete figure of few lobes will result, as shown, by the one design in lower right-hand corner of the illustration. An elliptical guide wheel may be used with a very flexible belt tightener. The axis may be taken at one of the foci or at the intersection of the axis of the ellipse.

The most complicated adjustment is to mount the table on the face of another disc, table and disc revolving in opposite directions. It will go through a long series of changes without completing any figure, and then will repeat itself. The diameters may be made to vary from the fraction of an inch to as large a diameter as the size of the table permits. The designs given here were originally traced on drawing paper 6 in. square.

Remarkable and complex as the curves produced in this manner are, they are but the results obtained by combining simultaneously two simple motions as may be shown in the following manner: Hold the table stationary and the pen will trace an oval. But if the guide wheel is secured in a fixed position and the table is revolved, a circle will result.

So much for the machine shown in *Fig. 1*. The number of the modifications of this simple contrivance is limited only by the ingenuity of the maker. *Fig. 2* speaks for itself. One end of the ruler is fastened in such a way as to have a to-and-fro motion over the arc of a circle, and the speed of the table is geared down by the addition of another wheel with a small pulley attached.

This will give many new designs. In *Fig. 3*, the end of the ruler is held by a rubber band against the edge of a thin triangular piece of wood that is attached to the face of the fourth wheel. By substituting other plain figures for the triangle, or outlining them with small finishing nails, many curious modifications such as are shown by the two smallest designs in the illustrations may be obtained. It is necessary, if symmetrical designs are to be made, that the fourth wheel and the guide wheel have the same diameter.

In *Fig. 4, V* and *W* are vertical wheels that may be successfully connected with the double horizontal drive wheel if the pulley between the two has a wide flange and is set at the proper angle. A long strip of paper is given a uniform rectilinear motion as the string attached to it is wound around the axle, *V.* The pen, *P,* has a motion compounded of two simultaneous motions at right angles to each other, given by the two guide wheels. Designs such as shown as a border at the top and bottom of the illustration are obtained in this way. If the vertical wheels are disconnected and the paper fastened in place, the well-known Lissajou's curves are obtained. These curves may be traced by

SPECIMEN SCROLLS MADE ON THE WONDERGRAPH

various methods, but this arrangement is the simplest of them all. The design in this case will change as the ratio of the diameters of the two guide wheels are changed.

These are only a few of the many adjustments that are possible.

Frequently some new device will give a figure that is apparently like one obtained in some other way; yet, if you will watch the way in which the two are commenced and developed into the complete design, you will find they are formed quite differently.

The average girl will take delight in making a wondergraph and in inventing the many variations that are sure to suggest themselves to her. It will not be time thrown away. As the contrivance is, it will arouse latent energies that may develop along more useful lines in later years.

— SMALL HAND LOOM DELIGHTS THE YOUNGSTERS —

Dollhouse rugs, pot holders, and dish pads of embroidery thread, yarn, or ordinary cotton string are but a few of the many practical items that any girl can weave on this simple hand loom. White pine is suitable for the frame, but the "heddle" cylinder, which raises the warps alternately by merely reversing the position of the handle with each pass of the shuttle, should be made from a maple or birch dowel. The cylinder, slotted as detailed on the next page, is made to pivot in slots cut in the rabbeted edge of the frame, and grooves cut lengthwise in the dowel. The edge of the shuttle is held in these cuts, serving to guide it easily between the warps. The frame is strung with heavy shoemakers' thread by securing the end around pins at

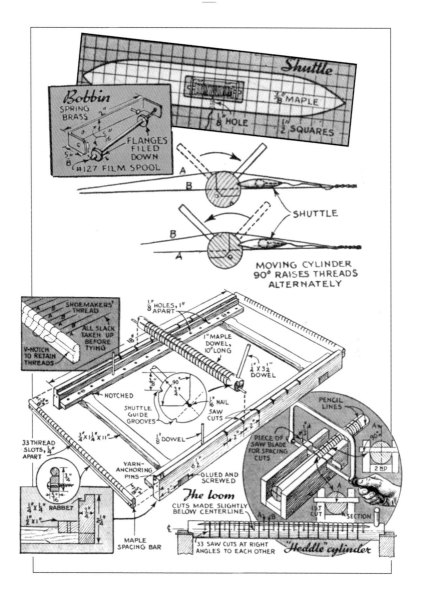

Shuttle
⅜ MAPLE
⅛" HOLE
½" SQUARES

Bobbin
SPRING BRASS
¾"
¹⁄₁₆"
⅝"
FLANGES FILED DOWN
#127 FILM SPOOL

A
B
SHUTTLE

B
A
SHUTTLE

MOVING CYLINDER 90° RAISES THREADS ALTERNATELY

SHOEMAKERS' THREAD
ALL SLACK TAKEN UP BEFORE TYING
V-NOTCH TO RETAIN THREADS
⅛"

⅛" HOLES, 1" APART
1" MAPLE DOWEL, 10" LONG
¼ X 3½" DOWEL

NOTCHED
⅜"
90°
3½"
¾"
SHUTTLE GUIDE GROOVES
⅛" NAIL SAW CUTS

⅜" DOWEL
2" 2" 2"

33 THREAD SLOTS, ¼" APART
¾" X 1¼" X 11"
YARN-ANCHORING PINS
GLUED AND SCREWED
The loom
CUTS MADE SLIGHTLY BELOW CENTERLINE

PENCIL LINES
90°
2 ND

PIECE OF SAW BLADE FOR SPACING CUTS
A
1ST CUT
SECTION

¾"
⁵⁄₁₆"
RABBET
¼" X ¼"
½" X 1"
¾"
2¼"
MAPLE SPACING BAR

33 SAW CUTS AT RIGHT ANGLES TO EACH OTHER
"Heddle" cylinder
A B

one corner and then spreading it into corresponding slots in the end rails and cylinder. Dowel pins are inserted upright in holes drilled equidistantly apart, in strips fitted along the inside of the frame. These serve to keep the work uniform in width and are advanced as the weaving progresses. A common film spool will serve for the shuttle bobbin.

— CAST BOOKENDS —

Casting bookends from her hands is one way to commemorate a little girl's precious years. It costs little, and your friends are sure to be intrigued by a life-size reproduction of a youngster's own hands, supporting a row of favorite books.

Producing a pair of these personalized bookends consists of making a "splash" plaster mold directly from the person's hand. To do this, the hand is first coated with petroleum jelly, as in *Fig. 1,* which prevents the plaster from sticking. Then the hand is rested palm down on wax paper on

a flat surface. The hand is then covered to the wrist with a mixture of casting plaster, as shown in *Fig. 2.* This splash coating should be at least ½ in. thick all over. After allowing the plaster to harden for about 30 minutes, the hand is turned over and worked free by gently wiggling the fingers, as in *Fig. 3.* Do this carefully to avoid damaging the mold.

Next, the hand impression in the splash mold is coated with two or

FIRST, COAT
BOTH SIDES OF THE HAND
WITH PETROLEUM JELLY

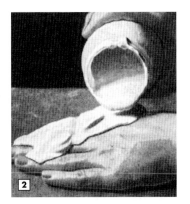

more applications of lacquer, as in *Fig. 4.* This seals the pores in the plaster and produces a glossy finish. This step is followed with a coat of paste wax which prevents the master pattern from sticking. The master pattern is made by merely filling the splash mold with plaster, the open end of the cavity being blocked off, as in *Fig. 5.* Because the splash mold is no longer needed, the master casting is removed by simply breaking

NEXT, REST THE HAND ON WAX PAPER AND COVER WITH PLASTER.

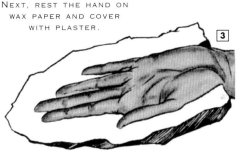

THE HAND IS FREED FROM THE PLASTER MOLD BY WIGGLING THE FINGERS.

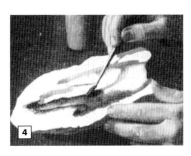

THE CAVITY OF THE MOLD IS PAINTED WITH TWO COATS OF LACQUER.

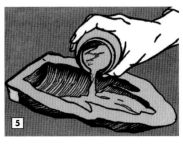

THE MASTER PATTERN IS MADE BY FILLING THE MOLD WITH PLASTER.

THE MOLD IS CAREFULLY CHIPPED
FROM THE MASTER WITH PLIERS.

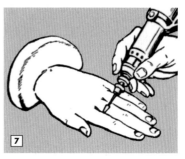

THE COMPLETED MASTER IS
CLEANED UP BY SANDING
THE FLAWS.

THE BASE IS ADDED TO THE
MASTER BY STANDING
IN WET PLASTER.

INGREDIENTS FOR THE MOLD ARE
COOKED IN A DOUBLE BOILER.

away small pieces of the mold with a pair of pliers, as shown in *Fig. 6*.

When this is done, a base is added to the hand. Pour plaster into a tin can to a depth of 1 in. While the plaster is still wet, place the master pattern upright in the can and embed it in the soft plaster, as in *Fig. 8*. Small holes from air bubbles and other irregularities in the master

ALCOHOL IS ADDED TO THE HOT MIXTURE.

RIGHT. MASTER AND SUBSEQUENT CASTINGS ARE EXTRACTED FROM THE MOLD BY STRETCHING IT.

casting can be corrected by sanding and patching where necessary. A small hand-grinder is a handy tool for cleaning up the pattern, as in *Fig. 7.* The portion of the base projecting on the flat side of the hand is carefully sawed off flush with the surface. Next, the master pattern is coated with lacquer.

The best material for creating the flexible mold is a silicone mold-making product, many of which are available at craft supply and hardware stores. A mold for the pattern can be made by removing both ends from a large can or by wrapping cardboard into a tube, as illustrated in *Fig. 12.*

The form should clear the pattern at least 1 in. all around. After pouring, the flexible mold is allowed to cure according to the package recommendations—many types allow you to control curing time for best results—before separating it from the pattern.

In preparation for making the finished casting, the flexible mold is dusted on the inside with talcum powder and left for an hour to allow any moisture in the mold to evaporate.

Low-temperature-melting materials that may be used to make finished

AN OPEN-END CAN PROVIDES
THE MOLD FORM.

castings include thermo-setting plastics, regular casting plaster, and other compounds that do not require heating the mold beyond 150° F. Before each casting is made, the mold cavity should be cleaned thoroughly with mold cleaner. Of course, only an adult should handle these materials or work with the mold that contains them. In addition to cleaning the mold surface, this mixture serves as a parting agent. In filling the mold, care should be used to pour the liquid down the side of the mold so that the lowest parts of the mold will be filled first, forcing any air bubbles to the top. Pouring should be done steadily without splashing. When the silicone flexible mold has served its purpose, it can be discarded.

Finish the bookends with pastel enamels or bronzing powders. A glaze-like finish in shiny black makes an attractive pottery-type casting. If plain plaster is used to cast the hand, it should be coated with shellac before painting, to seal the porous surfaces. Apply several coats of paint to build up a smooth heavy finish.

— HAND-CARVED "LAPELLIERES" —

Every girl likes jewelry for dress-up, especially brooches that will make that special outfit even more special. Here are fifteen novel dress-pin designs to carve in wood. All you need is a coping saw, a jackknife, and sandpaper.

These smart wooden dress ornaments are fun to carve and not at all difficult. The photos in *Fig. 1* make it easy for you to see just where to whittle and the right contours to duplicate. Patterns for the ornaments shown in *Fig. 1* are given on squares

AFTER SCROLL-SAWING A FIGURE
ROUGHLY TO SIZE, IT'S EASY TO
CARVE IT WITH A JACKKNIFE
AND SANDPAPER TO A
SMOOTH FINISH.

in *Fig. 2,* so that they can be readily enlarged for tracing on ³/₁₆-in. stock. Hardwoods, such as maple, walnut, mahogany, cherry, etc., are preferred to softwoods, because the cross grain is stronger and a higher polish can be achieved in finishing.

If you have a scroll saw, you can saw out as many as ten blanks of one kind at a time by stacking and nailing the layers together with brads. In carving, mouth and eyes are outlined with clean-cut V-grooves, while the contours are shaped by sloping the cut to meet a vertical one. For example, the squirrel's body and tail in *Fig. 1* are formed by the latter method, the eye being simply a deep V-cut accentuated with black ink.

The ornaments can be sanded or left rough-carved, and may be finished with several coats of hot linseed oil rubbed to a rich luster with a soft cloth. Or they can be finished with wax, shellac, or varnish. Toning provides still another variation for finishing the figures. For instance, the little fawn shown in *Fig. 6* can be

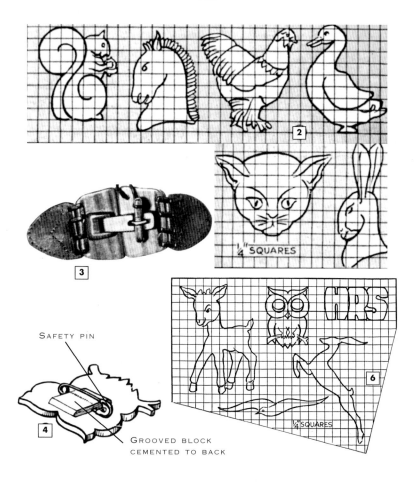

SAFETY PIN

GROOVED BLOCK
CEMENTED TO BACK

¼" SQUARES

two-toned by staining the hooves and nose black, and the upper part of the body and legs brown.

Fig. 4 shows how a common safety pin can be attached to the back of the figure to provide a suitable clasp, or clasps made for the purpose can be purchased. Monograms, *Fig. 6,* and belt buckles, *Fig. 3,* are other examples of what can be done.

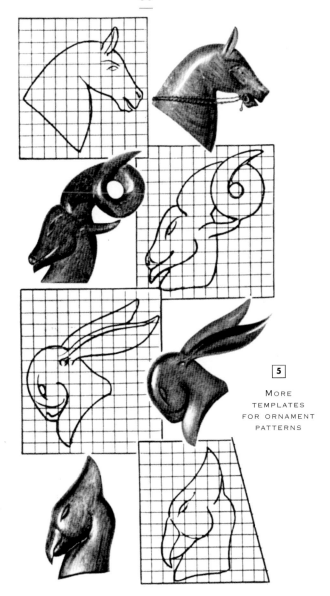

5

MORE
TEMPLATES
FOR ORNAMENT
PATTERNS

QUICK CRAFTS

— COLOR DESIGNS
WITH TRIANGLE BLOCKS —

Triangular blocks cut from fiberboard or plywood and colored, can be used in many ways for both practical purposes and entertainment. As a toy, the blocks will keep children engrossed for hours because the pieces may be combined into stars, arrows, strips and other shapes. The colored portions form designs within the shapes, as illustrated. Any number of triangles may be used, although twelve pieces are generally enough for most purposes. The blocks may be of any size, each one being divided by a line running through the apex and perpendicular to the base. Each block is painted red and white, blue and white, or blue and red. Four blocks of each color combination were used in most of the patterns shown here, but any other colors may be substituted.

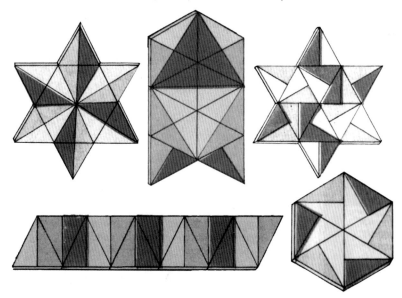

— Fun with Ink Pictures —

Fascinating ink pictures that will amuse youngsters for hours at a time can be made easily by the children themselves, using a few simple articles that are found in every home. However, before starting to make the pictures, it's wise to cover the table to be used with old butcher paper or newspapers, so that any ink that

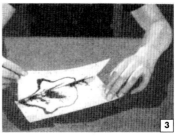

might be spilled accidentally will not mar the finish. If available, an old piece of oilcloth makes an ideal cover. The materials needed are several medicine droppers, as many kinds of colored ink as are available, and sheets of white and colored paper. Don't use paper that is too absorbent or too slick. The paper is folded, as in *Fig. 2,* and several

drops of ink are placed in the crease, as shown in *Fig. 1.* The paper is again folded on the crease and the ink is formed into patterns by running the fingers over the outside of the sheet. When it is opened, as in *Fig. 3,* the finished picture can be seen. Some of the pictures may resemble an animal or article of everyday life, while others may look

like creatures from another world. A greater variety is achieved by using several colors of inks. For example, red and green ink could be dropped on one sheet to make a two-colored picture. When using several colors, care should be taken that they do not run together and neutralize each other. Each new picture will differ somewhat from the ones that have been made, and this will hold the child's interest.

— MASKS FOR WALL PLAQUES MOLDED ON MODELED CLAY BASE —

Molding papier-mâché mask wall decorations, such as those shown in the illustrations, is a fascinating hobby that everyone can enjoy, as it is easy to do and costs very little. Materials needed are basic modeling clay, a few wooden blocks, some plastic sheeting, casein glue or white glue, shellac, and paper towels or newspapers.

Fig. 1 shows various suggestions for masks. Other styles can be made, as desired, but they are all made in the same way. First, wooden blocks are set on a base to provide a form over which the clay is pressed. The clay must be applied at least an inch thick to prevent cracking, *Fig. 3.* The blocks can be removed easily when the clay has dried. Next, features are molded

FIG. 1

with the fingers or with any handy small tool such as a skewer or awl, as in *Fig. 2.* After this, the model is left for about 24 hrs. When the clay is dry, vegetable oil or grease is applied all over, as in *Fig. 4,* and cloth is

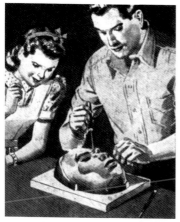

FIG. 2

pressed into all the contours, as shown in *Fig. 5*. Paper towels now are torn into small pieces and dropped into a pan of casein glue or white glue, as in *Fig. 6*. They are then laid on the cloth in three overlapping layers, as illustrated in *Fig. 7*, and allowed to dry. The moisture in the glue breaks down the fibers in the paper, leaving a skin-smooth, papier-mâché mask. The model is removed from the block form and the clay is picked out with an ice pick or other pointed tool, as in *Fig. 8*, without, of

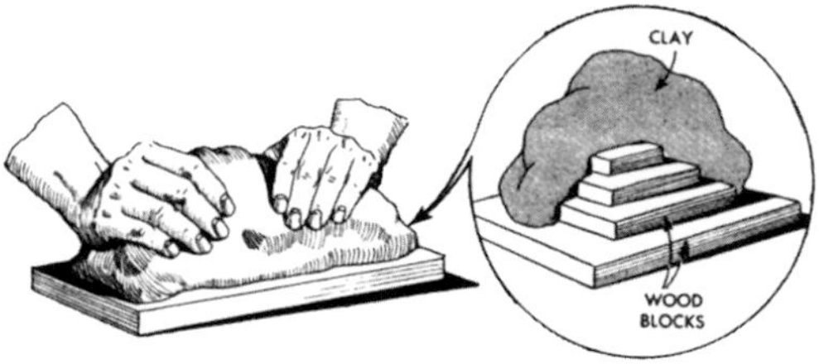

CLAY

WOOD BLOCKS

PAPER TOWEL

FIG. 3. CLAY PRESSED OVER BLOCKS

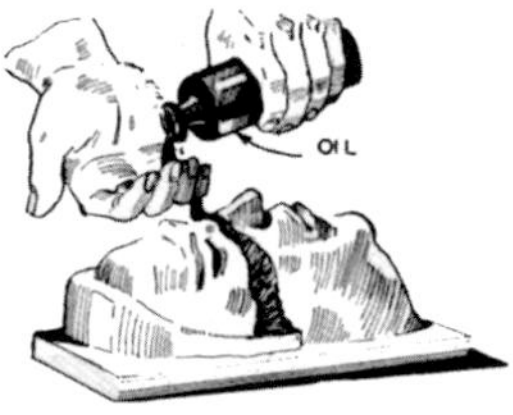

OIL

FIG. 4.
APPLYING OIL TO MODEL

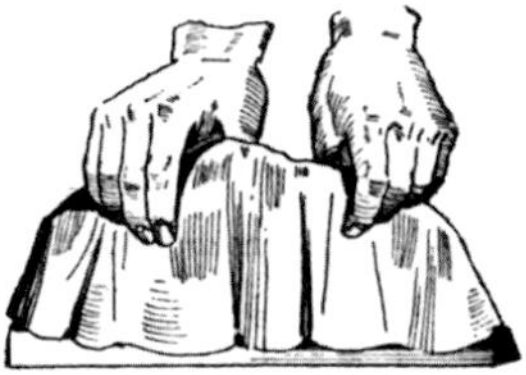

FIG. 5.
COVER WITH CLOTH.

GLUE

FIG. 6.
DROP PAPER TOWEL PIECES INTO GLUE.

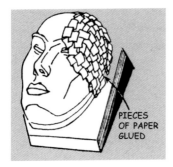

Fig. 7

PIECES
OF PAPER
GLUED

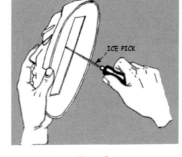

ICE PICK

Fig. 8

course, piercing the paper. Finally,
the mask is coated with shellac, as in
Fig. 9, and painted to suit. Gold or
silver paint can be applied, or green
poster color in a water-based gold
paint will give a bronze finish. Other
effects can be obtained with either
watercolors or oil paints.

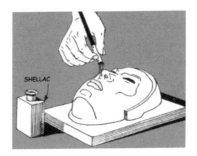

SHELLAC

Fig. 9

— FOLDING PAPER IS FUN FOR EVERYONE —

There is a real fascination for
little girls in taking nothing
more than a square piece of paper
and, by a few folds, producing a
bird that flaps its wings or a frog
that hops.

For the bird, use a piece of
heavy paper about 8 or 9 in.
square. First, the square is creased

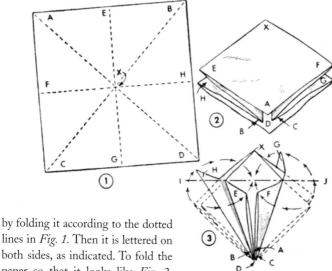

by folding it according to the dotted lines in *Fig. 1*. Then it is lettered on both sides, as indicated. To fold the paper so that it looks like *Fig. 2*, grasp corner B with the fingers of the right hand and corner C with the left and bring them together, allowing the paper to hinge or fold at point X. Then, holding these two corners with your left hand, bring up corners A and D. Lay the paper flat on the table with corners A, E, F, and X showing and crease all edges down flat. Some of the folds previously made will have to be reversed. Next bring edges AF and CF over to the crease line AX and crease. Do the same to edges AE and BE. Now turn the whole thing over and make similar folds by bringing corners H and

G to crease line DX. It should now look like F*ig. 3*, the arrows showing the direction of the folds. Next place the paper flat on the table with corner E and F showing and mark the pencil line IJ. Place the fingers of the right hand along the edge of the pencil line so that the palm covers point X and with the left hand fold corners E and F outward. Grasp corner A with the left fingers and fold and crease it at line IJ as shown by the arrows in *Fig. 4*. After this, fold corner A flat over corner X. Corners

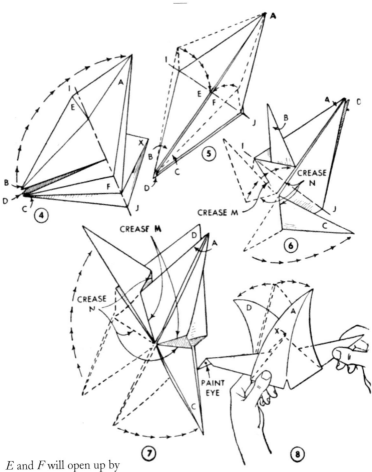

E and F will open up by
first swinging out and then
back again so that E and F will come
together in the center as shown in
Fig. 5. Turn the paper over and do
the same thing with corner D. Now
place the paper on the table with E

and F showing and following the
dotted lines and arrows in *Fig. 6.*
Fold tips C and B upward and outward to form crease N at approximately the same position and angle

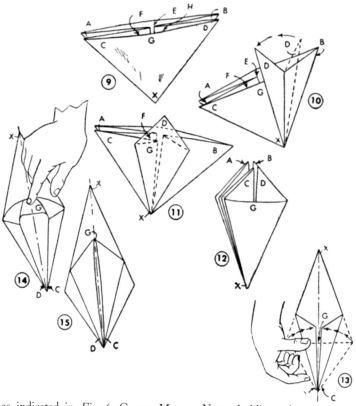

as indicated in *Fig. 6*. Crease *M*, extending from the inside corner formed by crease *N* to the outside corner of *IJ* line, is folded in a similar manner, except that the paper is folded upward and inward. Return tips *C* and *B* to their original positions, as the creases merely serve as guidelines.

Now, holding the paper in the left hand with *G* and *H* showing, you will find a small triangle between points *A* and *D*. Open the right-hand side of the triangle and with the right hand grasp the two edges of tip *C* just below crease *N* and move them upward as shown by the arrows in

Fig. 7. You will notice that creases *N* and *M* on one side of tip *C* will have to be reversed to allow crease *N* to be folded to the center between the two sides of the small triangle. Turn the paper around and do the same to tip *B*. Points *A* and *D* are curved downward to represent wings, while the protruding points form the neck and tail. Fold one of the extending tips to form the head and paint eyes on both sides. Holding the bird as shown in *Fig. 8*, the wings are made to flap realistically by pulling the tail.

A square folded and labeled as in *Fig. 1* is also used to make the hopping frog detailed in *Figs. 9* to *18*, inclusively. To fold the paper as in *Fig. 9*, grasp the creased line *H* with the right fingers and creased line *F* with the left fingers and bring them together, allowing the paper to fold at point *X*. Then, holding these corners with the left hand, bring up the crease lines *EG*. Lay the paper flat with corners *C*, *D*, and *X* showing, and crease all edges down flat. Notice that some of the folds will have to be reversed. Be sure the labeled crease lines are positioned as in *Fig. 9*. Edge *DX* is then folded over to align with crease line *GX*, *Fig. 10*. Crease this new fold, which is to serve as a guide crease when

folding as in *Fig. 11*. This is done by unfolding corner *D* to its original position. Then, holding the paper at corner *X* with the left hand, spread the two guide creases apart with the right hand, starting at corner *D*. Note that the left-hand guide crease has to be reversed. Now flatten the folded edge *DX* directly over the folded edge *GX*, shown as a dotted line in *Fig. 11*. Place the paper flat, as in *Fig. 11*, and lift up the right-hand guideline crease so that it hinges on the *DX* line and fold it over, placing it on top of the left-hand guideline crease. This exposes crease line *HX*. Edge *BX* is then folded over so it aligns with crease line *HX* and is creased to form guidelines. Then open up and form it as was done with corner *D*. Now turn the paper over to show corner *A* and crease line *EX* and repeat the above guide creasing and folding, first to corner *A*, then to corner *C*. Grasp the paper with the left hand at point *X* and fold over the right-hand guide-crease edge from right to left, exposing crease line *GX* and corners *C* and *D*, *Fig. 12*. Turn the paper over and repeat, exposing crease line *EX* and corners *A* and *B*.

The paper then is laid flat with point *X* away from you and corners

C and *D* showing. Now fold in the top right and left-hand unmarked corners to the center crease line *GX* and crease, as in *Fig. 13.* These two new folded edges are used as guide creases in the next step, which is somewhat similar to a process in making the bird. Draw a line across the newly formed right and left corners at right angles to the crease line *GX.* Then unfold them to their original positions and, with your right hand, lift up edge *G,* as in *Fig. 14,* and fold it back along the pencil line, which is creased as in making the bird. The cut edges of the paper will fold in to the center, after which the small kite-shaped folds are pressed flat against the paper, as in *Fig. 15.* Turn the paper over to show edge *E* and repeat the above process. Then locate edges *FH* and do the same thing.

Now hold the paper in your left hand with point *X* at the top and arrange the eight unmarked corners so that the small kite-shaped folds marked *G* are facing you and the ones marked *E* are at the back. The two lower tips facing you will be labeled *C* and *D,* the back two *A* and *B.* Lay the paper flat with *G* showing and fold the two upper right-hand unmarked corners to the center and

HOW TO MAKE A BELT.

crease the fold to taper to a point at tip C. Do the same to the two upper left-hand unmarked corners, and crease to tip D, as in *Fig. 16*. Turn the paper over, showing corner E, and repeat the above, folding and creasing to tips A and B. Then turn the paper over again and fold tips C and A, as in *Fig. 17*. Fold tips D and B so that they project out to the left. A smart tap on the back will make the frog in *Fig. 18* jump vigorously.

Any youngster can make a decorative belt out of heavy wrapping or colored craft paper. Sixty or seventy pieces of paper about 4½ by 2¼ in. are required. Each piece is folded lengthwise, as in *Fig. 19, A*, after which each edge is folded to the center crease, B. The ends of this strip

are brought together, C, to make the center crease. Then the ends are folded to this crease, as in D. This piece is joined to another, made the same way, by inserting the ends of the latter between the folds, E, and pulling both together firmly. Other pieces are added similarly to produce a belt of the required length.

The cap shown in *Fig. 20* is made from a double newspaper sheet. The size can be varied by increasing the size of the paper proportionally. To start, fold down the corners of the paper so that the edges meet, as at A. Then the second, third, and fourth folds are made, as at B, and the paper turned over before making the fifth fold at C. The latter is really two separate folds. After the sixth and

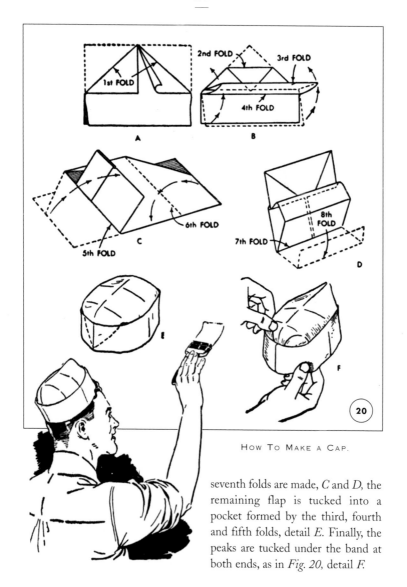

How To Make a Cap.

seventh folds are made, *C* and *D*, the remaining flap is tucked into a pocket formed by the third, fourth and fifth folds, detail *E*. Finally, the peaks are tucked under the band at both ends, as in *Fig. 20*, detail *F*.

— FIVE-POINTED STAR WITH ONE SNIP OF SCISSORS —

A perfectly proportioned five-pointed star can be cut from paper with a single cut of your scissors if the paper is folded four times as shown in *Figs. 1* to *5*. Ordinary 8½ by 11-in. paper, or other paper of the same proportions, is suitable. First, it is folded once through the middle, as shown in *Figs. 1* and *2*. Then the upper left-hand

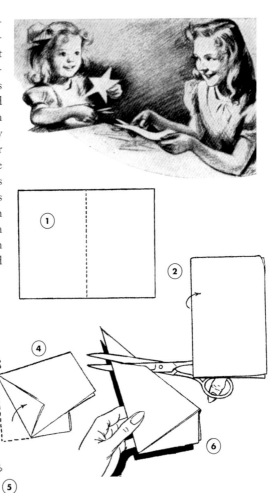

corner is brought down to the center of the bottom edge and the paper is folded, as in *Fig. 3.* Next, the lower left-hand corner is brought up and the paper is folded along the diagonal edge, as in *Fig. 4.* Finally, the right-hand edge is turned up to meet the left-hand edge, as in *Fig. 5,* or the right-hand portion can be folded under at the edge of the left-hand flap. Now the folded paper is cut, as in *Fig. 6,* and the cut-off portion will be the star. If long, narrow points are desired, the cut should be made at an acute angle, slanting toward the tip. A cut made more nearly straight across the paper will produce a star with blunter points.

— CORSAGES OF OILCLOTH, FELT, AND RAFFIA —

Artificial flowers that provide permanent corsages for the maturing girl's wardrobe are easy to make from simple materials that offer an endless variety of colors and combinations. For example, the daisy in *Fig. 1* is shaped from small pieces of oilcloth and fine wire. The five steps in forming it are detailed in *Fig. 2.* Note that the wire stem is looped over the slitted oilcloth before starting to roll the bud, and that the wire leaf stem is placed between the cutouts before pasting them together.

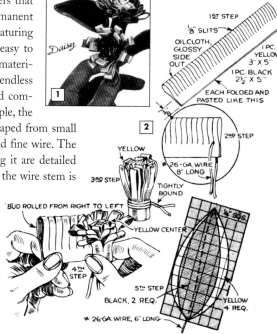

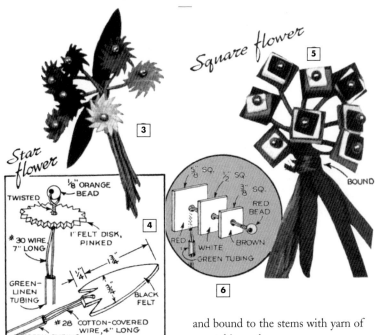

Square flower

5

Star flower

3

4

6

1/8" ORANGE BEAD

TWISTED

#30 WIRE 7" LONG

1" FELT DISK, PINKED

GREEN-LINEN TUBING

BLACK FELT

3/4"

1/4"

3/4"

#28 COTTON-COVERED WIRE, 4" LONG

GREEN TUBING

5/8" SQ. 1/2" SQ. 3/8" SQ.

RED BEAD

RED WHITE BROWN

GREEN TUBING

BOUND

The little bouquet of star flowers in *Fig. 3* shows what can be done with small pieces of felt and a few beads. Felt disks are best cut by following a cardboard pattern, after which the edges are pinked, as in *Fig. 4,* with sharp scissors or a razor blade. A similar bouquet of square flowers is shown in *Figs. 5* and *6*. These are assembled in the same manner as the star-shaped ones, with the exception of the leaves, which are ½-by-7-in. strips of felt, folded once and bound to the stems with yarn of a matching color.

Natural and red-colored raffia was used for the spiral flower, as in *Figs. 7* and *8,* although other materials, such as ribbon, string, or heavy yarn, could be used. Before starting to wrap the raffia, mark a straight line on the tube lengthwise. This will serve as a guide in keeping the 8-in. length of wire straight. In wrapping the stem, the wire ends are bent up and wrapping continued over them and back up the stem to cover any sharp edges. Use a large needle to slip the end of the raffia under the wrapping.

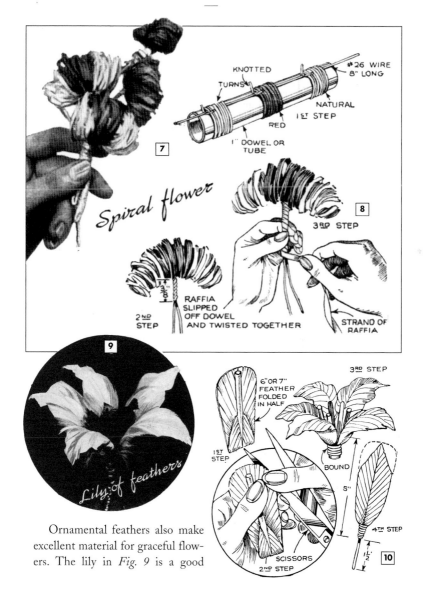

KNOTTED

TURNS

#26 WIRE 8" LONG

NATURAL

1ST STEP

RED

1" DOWEL OR TUBE

7

Spiral flower

3RD STEP

8

3/8

RAFFIA SLIPPED OFF DOWEL AND TWISTED TOGETHER

2ND STEP

STRAND OF RAFFIA

9

Lily of feathers

3RD STEP

6"OR 7" FEATHER FOLDED IN HALF

1ST STEP

BOUND

5"

4TH STEP

1½"

SCISSORS

2ND STEP

10

Ornamental feathers also make excellent material for graceful flowers. The lily in *Fig. 9* is a good example. For this, dyed chicken feathers were used to form the petals. While the center of the flower may be of the same color as the petals, a more striking effect is produced by using a contrasting color. Steps for shaping the feather petals are given in *Fig. 10*. After waving the edges with

scissors, the feathers are bent slightly outward by cracking the quill with the thumbnail every quarter inch. Short lengths of wire are wound with crepe paper and bound together. A tight wrapping of silk yarn, shown in *Fig. 11,* completes the stem covering.

— MAILING TUBE NOVELTIES —

You'll be surprised at the number of unusual and attractive novelties that can be made at practically no cost using just a few cardboard mailing tubes, some scrap wood, and a little ingenuity. Wax crayons and watercolors are used to decorate the novelties, after which they are finished with clear shellac to seal the colors. The four examples presented here show what can be done and will give you a start. Notice in each case that the novelty is built around a piece of mailing tube. Bases are of scrap wood and, if desired, you could incorporate plastic. If you have a lathe, you'll be able to turn out perfect disks for the bases in a jiffy, or you may find that you can do better

by cutting them on a scroll saw, sawing several at a time, and then smoothing the edges with sandpaper or a file. Choice pieces of scrap wood, such as walnut, maple or cherry, could be used and finished in their natural color with a coat of shellac or varnish. Quick-drying lacquers can be used to speed the painting. If you cover the paper tubes first with a thin wash coat of clear lacquer or shellac, the paint will not be absorbed as readily. Another finishing method is flocking. Flock can be had in a variety of colors and is simply sifted onto the work after it is coated with glue. The excess flock is shaken off and re-used. The finish obtained is a velvety texture resembling cloth and gives a professional looking job. Natural or dyed sawdust sprinkled on a tacky surface and pressed with your fingers will also give the work a novel finish.

CANDY AND NUT TRAY: What girl can resist candy by the wheelbarrow . . . especially when she's made the candy holder herself! A length of mailing tube, cut as shown and fitted with wooden ends, forms the hopper. The rest of the cart is made of scraps of ¼- and ½-in. pine. The wheel can be made to turn or it can be simply glued in the slotted end. Draw in the flower designs with yellow and red crayons and give the rest of the work a coat of yellow watercolor paint.

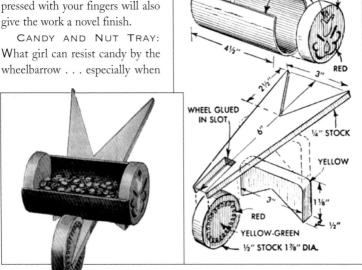

A WHEELBARROW CANDY HOLDER

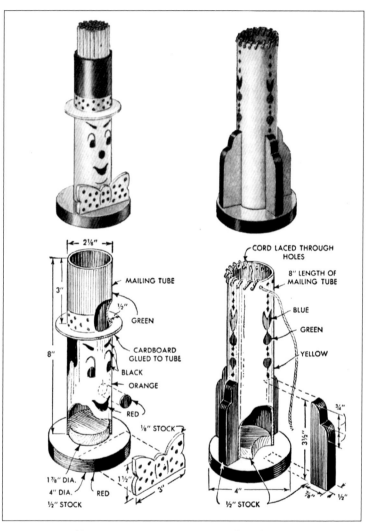

HOLDER FOR DRINKING STRAWS (LEFT) AND
ARTIFICIAL FLOWER VASE (RIGHT)

STRAW SERVER: (Opposite, left) Dapper Dan purposely "blew his top" to let you put soda straws in his stovepipe hat. Make him from a tube 8 in. long and see that the brim of his hat fits snugly around the tube, 3 in. from the top. He's attached to a circular base by a disk nailed to the top, and then dolled up with a sporty polka-dot tie. His features can be applied with a wax crayon and the rest done in watercolors. Finish with clear shellac and let dry.

ARTIFICIAL FLOWER VASE: (Opposite, right) Just the thing to hold paper flowers. You start by making a two-piece base like you did for the others. The tube sets over the top disk of the base and is glued or nailed to it. Four side supports are spaced equidistantly around the tube and fastened to the base with brads. Then holes are punched around the upper edge of the tube and laced with a cord to give a finish. Wax crayons color the side pieces. The tube is painted with watercolors.

— FUNNY FACES —

As favors at a girl's birthday party, these comic heads will bring squeals of delight—and they're so simple that any girl can make them. Using the same general idea, a

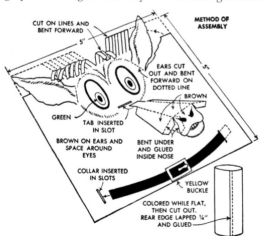

CUT ON LINES AND BENT FORWARD

5"

METHOD OF ASSEMBLY

EARS CUT OUT AND BENT FORWARD ON DOTTED LINE

BROWN

GREEN

TAB INSERTED IN SLOT

BROWN ON EARS AND SPACE AROUND EYES

BENT UNDER AND GLUED INSIDE NOSE

COLLAR INSERTED IN SLOTS

YELLOW BUCKLE

COLORED WHILE FLAT, THEN CUT OUT. REAR EDGE LAPPED ¼" AND GLUED

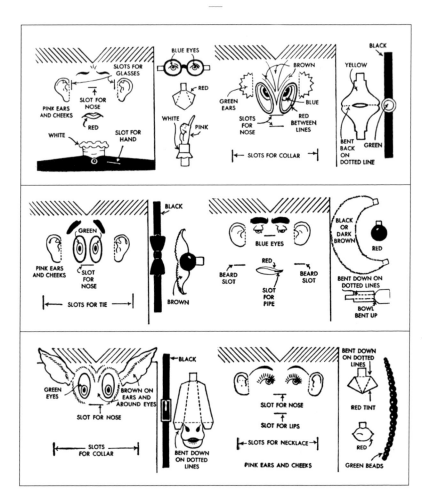

clever adult can fashion hilarious caricatures of friends to serve as entertaining place cards.

Using ordinary school drawing paper, and coloring with crayon or watercolor, a number of these original party favors can be turned out in a short time. Making them also affords an entertaining pastime for the youngsters who, after once getting the knack of it, can give free rein to their imaginations and artistic abilities. The first step is to mark off a sheet of paper in squares of the desired size, as shown in the illustration. Use a pencil and mark lightly so that the lines can be erased later without difficulty. Then draw the eyes, ears, nose, etc. with pen and ink or directly with color and completely color the design. Cut the head from the sheet as indicated by the solid vertical line and then cut out around the hair and ears. The ears are cut along the solid lines and folded forward along the dotted lines. Cut the necessary slots in the head and cut out the nose and accessories. Assemble and glue the ends of the head to form a cylinder.

— PIXY BANKS —

A great way to teach girls about the value of money and have a little one-on-one crafts time is to team up and make these wonderful little banks. Sections of mailing tube form the bodies of these little pixy banks, which can be made short or tall. Scraps of pine will do for the wooden parts. The squared drawing gives two different head patterns.

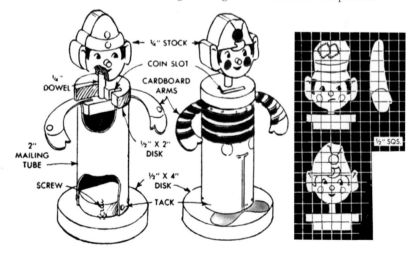

— How to Make Silhouettes —

Photography in all branches is truly a most absorbing occupation. Each of us who has a camera is constantly experimenting, and every one of us is delighted when something new is suggested for such experiments.

The process described assumes a camera that uses film as opposed to a digital model (although you can use the same process with a digital camera, just print out the result rather than develop it). Select a window facing north, if possible. Actually, any window will do if used only at a time when the sun is not on it. Raise the window shade halfway, remove any curtains there may be. In the center of the lower pane of glass, paste a sheet of thick, perfectly smooth tissue paper by the four corners, as shown in the sketch at *B*.

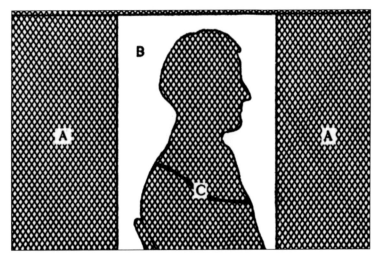

MAKING A SILHOUETTE WITH A CAMERA.

Darken all the rest of the window, shutting out all light from above and the sides. Place a chair so that after being seated, the head of the subject will be positioned in front of the center of the tissue paper, and as near to it as possible. When looking straight before the sitter, their face will be in clear profile to the camera.

Draw the shades of all other windows in the room. Focus the camera carefully, getting a sharp outline on the profile on the screen. Do not stop down the lens, because this makes long exposure necessary, and the subject may move.

Correct exposure depends, of course, on the lens, the light, and the film. But remember that a black-and-white negative is wanted with as little detail in the features as possible (so you'll be using black-and-white film). The best film to use is a very slow one.

In developing, get all possible density in the highlights, without detail in the face and without fog (or, if having the film developed, as the developer to do this). Printing is best done on contrast development paper with developer that is not too strong.

The ideal silhouette print is a perfectly black profile on a white ground. With a piece of black paper, any shape may be made, as shown at *C* in the sketch.

Jewelry Corner

— Holders for Earrings —

Every girl needs her own jewelry holders. That's why earring holders are an excellent project to tackle. These plastic earring holders are not only attractive and useful additions to the dressing-table, but each one is an especially interesting one-evening project for the crafter who likes to work with plastics. The first step in making either cutout is to enlarge the squared patterns to full size and transfer them to the protective paper covering on a sheet of 3/16-in. clear plastic. Then cut on the pattern lines with a hand or power jigsaw, using a fine-toothed blade. After sawing, go over the edges with a fine file to remove the saw marks. Now, polish the edges with a buffing wheel charged with rouge polishing compound. The wheel should be run at a slow speed

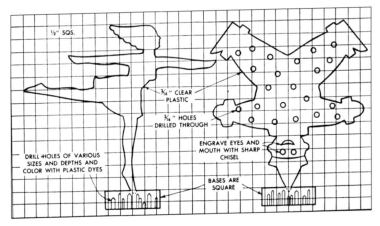

½" SQS.

¾₆" CLEAR PLASTIC

¾₆" HOLES DRILLED THROUGH

ENGRAVE EYES AND MOUTH WITH SHARP CHISEL

DRILL HOLES OF VARIOUS SIZES AND DEPTHS AND COLOR WITH PLASTIC DYES

BASES ARE SQUARE

because, otherwise, heat may soften the plastic. Note that the tip of the clown's hat and the dancer's toe are extended somewhat for attaching to plastic bases. These edges should be left square. Holes in the body, arms, and legs of the clown are drilled clear through. But the eyes, mouth

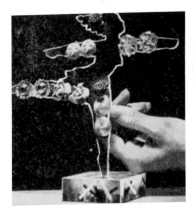

CLEAR PLASTIC IS USED FOR THIS CUTOUT AND BASE.

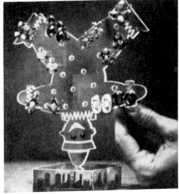

THIS CLOWN CUTOUT PROVIDES A NOVEL RACK FOR HANGING CLUSTERS OF COLORFUL EARRINGS.

and other lines are cut into the surface with a sharp-pointed tool. Holes also are drilled in the bases to varying depths with drills of different sizes. The holes are filled with plastic dye and, after allowing time for the dye to color deeply, the excess is drained out. The eyes of the clown are dyed blue and the mouth red. When the cutouts are finished, force the dancer's toe and the tip of the clown's hat into shallow holes drilled in the bases and cement in place.

— TRINKET CHEST —

The trick lid on this attractive burnt-cypress trinket chest will foil the tiny prying hands of a younger sibling because instead of opening in the conventional manner, the lid is pivoted on parallel arms

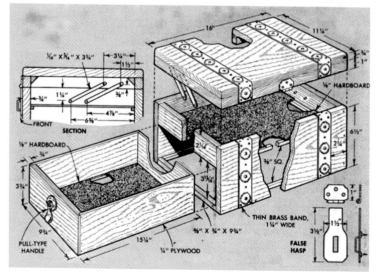

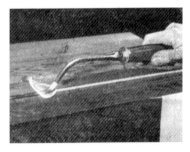

"SUGI" FINISH IS PRODUCED BY CHARRING THE CYPRESS AND THEN BRUSHING WITH A FINE-WIRE BRUSH TO RAISE THE GRAIN.

A TWO-PIECE DUMMY HASP PARTS WHEN THE LID IS PULLED UP AND ADDS TO THE DECEPTION OF HOW THE LID WORKS.

and must be pulled forward. The "sugi" or burnt-wood finish is produced by charring the wood lightly and rubbing it with a suede-shoe brush to bring out the grain in relief. A wash coat of thin, clear lacquer containing gilt is applied, then immediately wiped off.

— NOVELTY JEWELRY FROM SHEET METAL —

Many attractive and unusual articles of jewelry, such as napkin clasps and rings, bracelets, pins, and brooches, can be made from small pieces of sheet metal. The work is learned easily, requires only a few common hand tools, and provides unlimited opportunity for originality in design. A grown-up can help a young girl to execute her designs, while the older girl will be able to handle much of the crafting work herself. In addition to adding to the girl's wardrobe, novelty jewelry

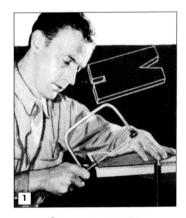

SAWING THE METAL

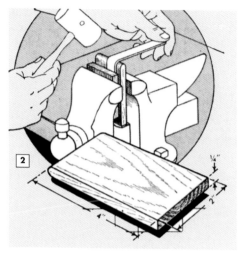

CLAMP THE SCROLLED END
AND SHAPE THE CLASP OVER A BLOCK.

NAPKIN CLASPS: These popular and useful articles are not only the easiest to make, but illustrate the procedures to be followed in fashioning the more difficult pieces. Cut a strip 2 by 5¼ in. from a sheet of 16-gauge aluminum or German silver, using tin snips, as in *Fig. 13.* A design such as one of those shown in *Fig. 3,* is drawn on paper, which is cemented to the metal strip. Shellac or rubber cement can be used as an adhesive.

makes ideal gifts for Mom, sisters, other relatives, and friends.

Materials: Half-hard aluminum, soft brass, cold-rolled copper, German silver, nickel and many other metals and alloys are suitable. The thickness, or gauge, of the metal depends on the article to be made. For napkin clasps and rings, 16-gauge is suitable, but for pins and other ornamental items, metal as light as 36-gauge—a little less than 1/64 in.—can be used.

When this has dried, the metal is trimmed down roughly to the shape of the design, then scroll-sawed to finish size. For sawing, a notched and slotted board is used, as in *Fig. 1.* The board is clamped to the workbench and the metal is positioned so that the lines to be sawed are over the notched cutout. The work should be held firmly on the cutting board to prevent vibration while being sawed, because this may cause the blade to break. With the blade teeth pointing toward the handle, the saw is tilted forward slightly except when cutting a sharp corner.

This must be done slowly to allow the blade to clear away enough stock to turn without binding or breaking. Wax rubbed on the blade will serve as a lubricant so that it will cut freely.

When using a design like that shown in the right-hand detail of *Fig. 3*, portions of the metal must be sawed out. This is done by first drilling small holes through which the saw blade can be inserted. The work is clamped between two wood blocks as in *Fig. 5*, so that the drill will cut through the metal without damaging the workbench. The locations of the holes should be center-punched before drilling so that the drill will not slip out of place and scratch the metal.

After all sawing has been done, the edges are smoothed by draw-filing. The work is held in a vise between two blocks of wood, which are placed about ⅛ in. below the edge of the work to give greatest support to it. A small mill file is then gripped with both hands and drawn flat in one direction only along the edge of the metal. Because aluminum and other soft metals clog a file quickly, chalk should be rubbed on the file frequently to prevent it's filling up. When all edges have been filed smooth, they should be rubbed down with a strip of medium emery cloth followed by a strip of No. 0 cloth.

The metal is polished with a fine abrasive such as powdered pumice or ordinary kitchen scouring preparations applied with a damp cloth. Fine steel wool can be used to produce a dull, rich finish, but for a bright luster, jeweler's rouge or metal polish, such as that

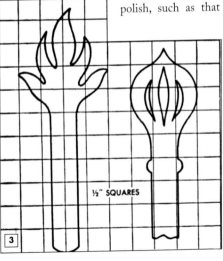

½" SQUARES

3

THE TEMPLATE

used on automobiles, can be applied with a felt pad. Then paste wax is rubbed on to protect the finish. Or lacquer, which is more durable, is applied with a small brush.

To shape the clasp, the scrolled end is clamped between two blocks in a vise, as in *Fig. 2*, the end of one block being rounded to assure a uniform curve when the metal is bent over it. When shaping the clasp, push down gradually with one hand and tap it lightly with a mallet.

NAPKIN RING: The napkin ring in *Fig. 7* is made in the same way as the clasps, although a differently

DRILLING THE METAL

shaped forming block is used. Monograms and initials, which may be varied to suit individual requirements for decorating the ring, are

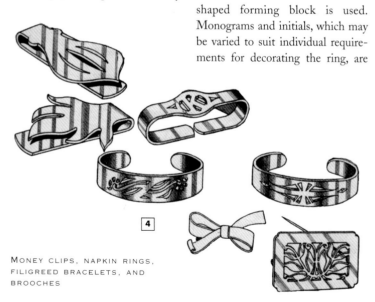

MONEY CLIPS, NAPKIN RINGS, FILIGREED BRACELETS, AND BROOCHES

illustrated in *Fig. 9*. Before shaping and polishing the ring, its entire surface—or a small portion of it—can be hammered to produce a pleasing effect. This is done by tapping the surface lightly with a ball-peen hammer, or by indenting the surface with a punch made by rounding one end of a short length of ⅜-in. dowel. To bend the ring, a line is marked on one side of the forming block across its center, and the strip of metal, after being scroll-sawed, filed, and polished, as previously explained, is positioned over it so that half its length extends on each side of the line. The strip, of course, must be aligned carefully along the edges of the block so that, when bent, the

ends will meet exactly. Then the strip is covered with a small wooden block and clamps are tightened over the work. After which the ends are bent and tapped with a mallet until the ring is formed.

FILIGREED BRACELETS: Although they are made in much the same way as the napkin rings, the bracelets shown in *Fig. 11* require a little more experience because of the intricacy of their designs and the small portions to be sawed out. Nickel or German silver is preferable to brass, copper or aluminum for making bracelets. These are formed over the end of an anvil. When doing this work, care must be taken to avoid distorting the web pieces of the

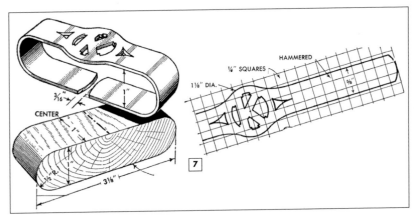

NAPKIN RING AND FORMING BLOCK.

design. For this reason, a thin metal strip is laid over the work to protect it while it is tapped with a mallet, as indicated in the lower left-hand detail of *Fig. 11.*

PINS AND BROOCHES: Several kinds of pins and brooches are shown in *Figs. 8, 12,* and *14.* For the filigree-type brooch in *Fig. 8,* 20-gauge silver or German silver is suitable. When sawing metal of this thickness, it is best to use the slotted end rather than the notched end of the sawing board, as shown in *Fig. 1,* so that the work will be well supported. If the piece buckles under the saw, the kinks may show even after the piece is straightened again. Such defects are enough to ruin the material for this purpose. A regular pin back with safety catch, available at jeweler's supply houses and craft shops, is soldered on the back.

The bowknot pin in *Fig. 12* is light enough to be worn on a blouse, because it is made from 36-gauge silver or German silver, which is cut with small tin snips. Before bending the cutout strip according to the cross-hatched pattern, one side can be polished to a high gloss and the other side can be rubbed to a dull, satin finish. This way when the strip is folded as indicated in the upper

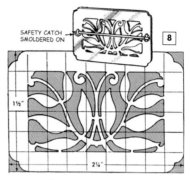

A FILIGREE BROOCH

left-hand details, the alternating gloss and satin finish will give a pleasing, silky appearance. After bending the strip, a band of heavier

stock is wrapped around the center and soldered at the back. A pin back may now be soldered in place. If the pin is made of aluminum, a strip of brass, cut and shaped as shown in the right-hand details, can be used instead. The brass strip is provided with a slot through which the ends of the band are slipped and pinned to hold them in place.

Silhouettes of animals, as in *Fig. 14,* are always popular as pins, but trees, leaves, or sketches adapted from illustrations can also be used. Copper or brass is

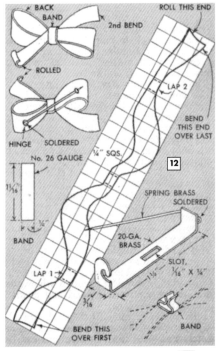

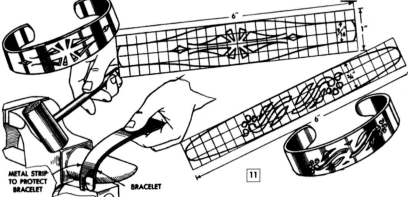

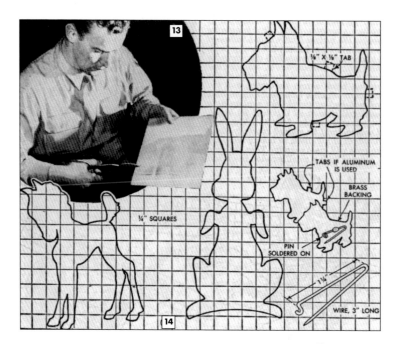

In the diagram: ½" X ½" TAB · TABS IF ALUMINUM IS USED · BRASS BACKING · ¼" SQUARES · PIN SOLDERED ON · WIRE, 3" LONG · 1¼" · 13 · 14

attractive, although aluminum is also satisfactory. However, if aluminum is used, the pin fastening cannot be soldered to the back unless special solder is used. Instead, tabs should be provided for folding over a brass backing to which the pin can be attached, as indicated in the right-hand details of *Fig. 14.* If a pin back or pin mounting is not available, one can be improvised from a length of spring wire, or an ordinary safety pin may be substituted.

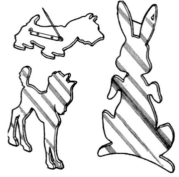

ANIMAL SHAPES FASHIONED
INTO BROOCHES

— "BEEHIVE" JEWELRY BOX HAS TWO COMPARTMENTS —

A pleasing beaded exterior distinguishes this little jewelry box from most turned boxes. Each compartment is of such size that jewelry can be seen and picked out easily. The lower compartment holds necklaces and brooches while the tray is convenient for rings. There are four operations in this turning job. First, the inside of the lower half is turned out. Second, the inside of the top half is turned out to match the lower half. Third, the two halves are fitted together, placed between lathe centers and the exterior is

turned as one piece, which assures continuity of line. In this operation, the beading is done. Fourth, the false bottom or tray is turned to fit.

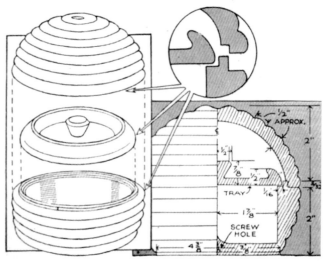

— Beads for Paper Necklaces —

Paper beads can readily be made with the aid of the simple device shown in the illustration. It consists of a base upon which a winding mechanism is mounted. This comprises a hand crank connected to a ⅜-in. shaft held in a flat-iron bracket; a split needle, which is engaged with the end of the shaft; a wooden support for the needle, which can be swung outward as indicated by the dotted lines; and a tray for holding paste or glue. The split needle is a ¼-in. rod, and the end is squared to fit snugly into a hole in the end of the shaft, which makes it easy to remove. A small gear is fitted to the end of the shaft to engage with a larger gear on the crank arm. The beads are made from tapered strips of paper, which can be cut from the colored pages of magazines. The

BEAD-WINDING DEVICE
FACILITATES MAKING
PAPER NECKLACES.

wide end is inserted in the split needle. A few turns of the crank will wind the whole strip into a compact roll. The end is dipped into the glue before it is wound on. The bead is then removed and given a coat of white shellac. The size and shape of the beads can be varied by varying the width and length of the paper strips.

HOLIDAY FAVORITES

— FAVORS AND CENTERPIECES FOR AN EASTER PARTY —

Easter brings with it the call to spring and a chance to celebrate the season with a party! It's easy to make these appropriate favors and table decorations for Easter. The humorous trio pictured in *Figs. 1, 2, and 3* are made from empty eggshells; hard-boiled eggs may also be used.

The pig in *Fig. 1* has paper ears, a macaroni-ring snout, date legs, ink dots for his spots and eyes, and a yarn tail. Perched atop an inverted bottle cap, the alert little squirrel is made from a brown-shelled egg or one dyed brown. His tail consists of a 4-in. strip of brown paper, fringed and curled. His ears are cut from the same material, and the features are inked on. The grinning clown utilizes an empty eggshell and owes his upright position to a small stone that was dropped gently through the hole made for removing the egg contents.

The peaked paper cap gives him a saucy air and effectively hides the hole. He has a dot nose and India-ink eyes and mouth.

Appearing real enough to cuddle, the bunny in *Fig. 4* is made from paper and cotton. Use soft pastel matt stock for the folder, cutting a strip 5 by 10 in. Fold the strip at the center and then fold back the ends to form a support. Make a bunny cutout in the front of the folder and glue a pad of cotton to the inside back of it. Then glue the edges together. The cotton will fluff out through the cutout to make a realistic looking bunny. Use pink felt, flannel, or paper for the eye and shape a nest from a few wisps of colored excelsior. The dignified little bunny centerpiece in *Fig. 5* is made from a salt carton covered with white felt, flannel, or paper. The ears and feet are cut from the same material. Eyes and nose should be bits of pink material. Give him a dainty pink or blue necktie of ribbon or yarn. If desired, the bottom may be removed from the carton and tiny favors or gifts placed inside.

— Rainbow Eggs for Easter —

By mounting the shell of an old brass lamp socket on the spindle of your child's phonograph, you can make a spinning hold for "striping" Easter eggs. Use a regular insulating bushing to make sure of a snug fit. The set screw will hold it in place and prevent wobbling. Before you begin coloring eggs, cover the turntable with heavy brown wrapping paper to catch any dye that might drip. Then perch an egg upright in the socket and set the phonograph at slow speed. By holding a brush moistened with dye against the egg, you can produce a simple striped design.

For a rainbow effect, load the brush slightly heavier with dye and change colors frequently. With practice, you can create many novel effects.

— SAFE JACK-O'-LANTERN —

Inserting a flashlight in the mouth of a paper bag is an easy way to make a perfectly safe jack-o'-lantern that will delight young-sters. Select a large paper bag, preferably white, and paint a comical face on one or both sides. Then insert the flash-light, leaving the switch exposed, and tie it in place with string or ribbon.

— TWO CHRISTMAS TOYS: HOPPING RABBIT AND WALKING DUCK —

There is no need for a big sister to spend her hard-earned money on toys for gifts. With a little help, she can create one-of-a-kind toys for kids that will be bet-ter than anything offered in the stores. Common materi-als and just a few tools are required for the construction of the toys described here. The first is a hopping rabbit in which an eccentric axle attached to the hind legs gives motion to the body as the toy is pulled along.

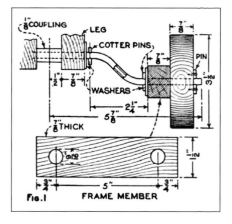

The rear axle of the toy, as in *Fig. 1,* is made from two pieces of ⅛-in. pipe bent to give the 1-in. offset. The axle is threaded at the inside ends, where they are joined between the rear feet, with a ⅛-in. pipe coupling. This construction allows the toy to be assembled after

A scroll saw or band saw is needed to cut out the body and legs. The approximate form of the body is obtained by dividing an 8 by 10-in. sheet of paper into 1-in. squares and sketching the shape, following *Fig. 2* closely. A paper pattern may be cut and used as a guide in the layout of the body, or the layout may be done directly on the 1-in. board chosen for the body. The material for body and legs should be close-grained and free from knots and cracks. The two pairs of legs are laid out in a manner similar to that followed in shaping the body. The location of the pivot points for the legs is given in

the axle pieces have been bent. The legs are kept from working out on the axle by ½-in. plain washers, secured by small cotter pins. The front axle is a straight piece of ⅛-in. pipe, of the same overall length as the assembled rear axle.

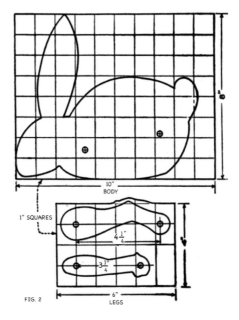

8"

10"
BODY

1" SQUARES

4¼"

3¼"

FIG. 2

6"
LEGS

TEMPLATE FOR THE HOPPING RABBIT

the illustration. The holes at the feet have a diameter of $^9/_{16}$ in., while those at the upper ends are large enough to accommodate ¼-in. bolts.

A frame member on each side of the toy spaces the axles to a distance of 5-in. from center to center. These members are assembled just inside of the wheels, and are kept in place by washers secured by cotter pins. Clear-grained wood wheels, with a diameter of 3½ in., are slipped on just outside of the frame members. The wheels are kept in place by washers and cotter pins on the front axle. But at the rear of the toy, the axle is made to turn with the wheels by omitting the washers outside of the wheels. A staple on each side of the axle will hold the cotter pins tightly.

The rear legs are pivoted to the body with an ordinary ¼-in. bolt. A washer, placed between each of the legs and the body, helps to reduce friction. The front legs are fastened

the lettering is inked, making the sentiment expressed suit the picture used, as shown in the illustrations. From this, a copy the exact size of the desired card, is taken, and prints made. These should be mounted on rough cover paper, contrasting in color with the print.

The lettering may be printed in white by cutting through the original print, laying it over white paper before making the copy.

It is best to make the card prints on double-weight, linen-finish buff or white paper. It's also wise to make the prints to suit a particular size of envelope, as it is usually easier to do this than to find an envelope to suit the print.

Should any difficulty be encountered in making the prints stay flat, dampen the backs, and put them between blotters under a weight, and allow them to dry.

— SAY IT WITH CHRISTMAS CARDS —

It's fun making your own Christmas cards and the result is emphatically "greetings by you"—not a cold substitute purchased over the counter. Artistic ability is required for some of these cards; others demand no more skill than the ability to paste two pieces of paper together.

Let's start with linoleum-block prints. The printing plate is a suitable square of battleship linoleum, and on this is tooled the image of the picture that is to ornament the card. Tools for this purpose, together with a little booklet on how to do it, can be purchased from art supply houses

INKING THE PLATE

or crafts stores. After the plate has been made, it is inked with printers' ink, as shown in *Fig. 1* above. The block is then placed in a book press, the paper is laid over it, and the clamp is turned down tightly to make the impression. Lacking a

book press,
you can get
nice impressions with the simple
press detailed in *Figs. 7* and *8*. The
side pieces hold the plate in position
and are about 1/64 in. below the level
of the plate. The flap is a piece of
felt, sheet rubber or cardboard. The
impression is made by
turning the flap down
and rubbing with a
rolling pin, as in *Fig. 7*.
Typical examples of
block printing are
shown in *Figs. 2* to *6*.

You can work won-
ders with paper cutouts
created using a scroll
saw, as illustrated in

Figs. 9 to *11* inclusive. A suitable
design is first drawn on paper that is
cemented to a 1/8-in. piece of wood.
A similar piece is used on the bottom of the "pad" with 30 to 50
sheets of paper between the two. See
Fig. 10. The design is then cut on a
scroll saw, resulting in a complete set

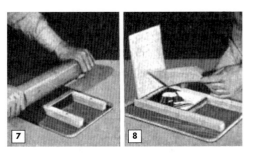

A SIMPLE PRESS FOR BLOCK PRINTING

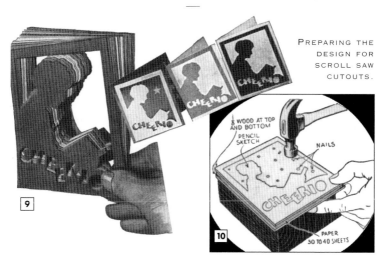

PREPARING THE DESIGN FOR SCROLL SAW CUTOUTS.

of paper cutouts. Three applications of this cutout are shown in *Fig. 9.* One is a glazed black card with a short fold, the cutout being tipped on the short fold. Another shows a single fold of cream-colored paper, on which is tipped a square of red metallic paper on which is tipped the cutout. The third is a cutout in reverse. That is, the cutout in this case is the portion discarded in the other examples. The cutout is of silver paper and it is tipped on a black card. The lettering is "spatter work," applied by using a stencil and then spattering the color on with a toothbrush as shown in *Fig. 11.* In *Fig. 12* to 14, the Christmas tree, the moon,

SPATTER THE COLOR ON WITH A TOOTHBRUSH.

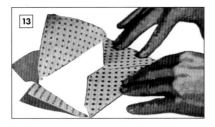

and the word "Noel" are cut out on the scroll saw. The edge of the tree is outlined with white and the tree cutout is backed with green metallic paper, while the moon and "Noel" are backed with red metallic paper.

Now we will consider something else: Envelopes . . . and paper. Ordinary stationery in tint colors often can be adapted for greeting-card use, and in this case you would have paper and envelopes to match. However, it's no trick to make your own envelopes, and by using decorative papers you can add a lot to the smartness of the card. *Fig. 14* shows various envelope styles. A cardboard pattern should be made so that the outline can be transferred quickly to the paper and cut out. Envelopes should be ⅛ in. larger than cards. Folding is done over a square of cardboard, as shown in *Fig. 13.* The edges can be cemented, or Christmas seals can be used for this purpose. The paper for cards can be almost anything. Colored Bristol board is excellent and easily

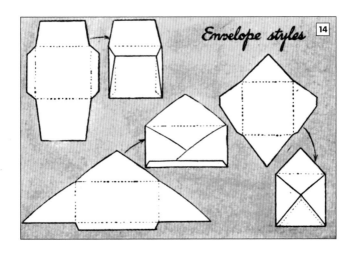

Envelope styles

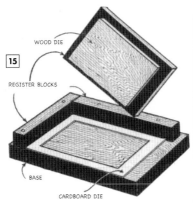

A SIMPLE HOMEMADE PRESS FOR EMBOSSING (LEFT) AND EMBOSSING THE CARD (RIGHT)

obtainable. Construction paper (the kind that children use in schoolwork) is sold almost everywhere and can be obtained in all the colors of the rainbow. Its one fault is that it has a full soft finish. This can be remedied in many cases by using jackets of cellophane. Decorative paper for cards and envelopes can be obtained from craft stores. For other kinds of paper, see local printers. If you like to emboss cards, you can use the simple homemade press shown in *Figs. 15* and *16*. The dies are made of wood and cardboard, and should be registered accurately so that the top die fits neatly within the bottom one. Paper placed between the two dies and hammered will be embossed neatly.

The dies will hold up nicely for about forty impressions. Embossing adds considerably to the card when block prints, photos or printed slips are to be tipped in.

A simple scroll idea that is a bit different is shown in *Fig. 17*. It is mailed in a small tube covered with decorative paper. *Fig. 18* shows a new idea—two pieces of wallboard covered with decorative paper and hinged together like the covers of a book. An amusing application of a

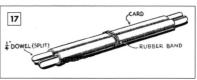

A SIMPLE SCROLL

WALLBOARD COVERED WITH DECORATIVE PAPER AND HINGED LIKE A BOOK
(LEFT), AND A BLOCK PRINT MOUNTED ON A WALLPAPER SCRAP (RIGHT)

block print mounted on a roughly torn piece of wallpaper, is shown in *Fig. 19*. Underneath the cut is the inscription "We tore the paper off the walls to send you Christmas Greetings ..." The same idea could be applied to oilcloth from the kitchen table and also to old newspaper or magazine pages.

Fig. 21 is an example of an easily made photographic card made from five snapshots, one of which is shown in *Fig. 20*. These snaps are cut out and mounted on a piece of white cardboard. Rephotographing gives the finished photo from which the cards are printed. All lettering is done on the pasted-up layout before copying.

A PHOTOGRAPHIC CARD

{ CHAPTER 2 }

DIVINE DOLLHOUSES

—

LIVING *in* STYLE

— A COLONIAL MANSION DOLLHOUSE —

This beautiful eight-room dollhouse is a replica of a colonial mansion complete with electric lights, fireplace and an open stairway. Both ends swing open for access to rooms upstairs and down, as shown on the next page. Made of plywood, the house measures 31½ by 44¾ in., exclusive of porches and bal-

cony. The rear stoop and front porch are detachable to permit the house to be carried through a 32-in. opening. If it is to be carried through a doorway of smaller width, the dollhouse must be reduced.

EACH SIDE GIVES ACCESS TO ROOMS
UPSTAIRS AND DOWN.

SIDE WALLS ARE HINGED TO OPPOSITE
CORNERS OF THE HOUSE.

The first step is to make the base framework, as shown in *Fig. 3*. Pieces of solid stock, ¾ by 1¾ in., are used and are assembled with the pieces set on edge. Then the frame is floored with five pieces of ¼-in. plywood, spaced as shown in *Fig. 4* to form ¼-in. grooves into which the interior walls are fitted. The second-floor frame, *Fig. 5*, is built-up similarly, except that the frame members are placed flatwise, and wider cross members are installed for walls *E* and *F* (shown in *Fig. 10*). Both sides of

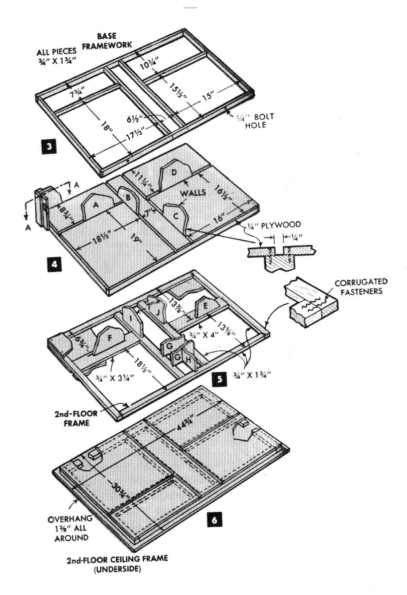

BASE FRAMEWORK

ALL PIECES
¾" X 1¾"

10¼"

7¾"

15½"   15"

6½"

18"   17½"

¼" BOLT HOLE

3

A

WALLS   16½"

8¾"   11¼"   D

A   B

7"   C

18½"   19"   16"

¼" PLYWOOD   ¼"

4

CORRUGATED FASTENERS

13⅞"

I   J   E

F   13⅝"

6¾"   ¾" X 4"

G

G   H

18½"   ¾" X 1¾"

¾" X 3¼"

5

2nd-FLOOR FRAME

44¾"

30¾"

OVERHANG 1⅜" ALL AROUND

6

2nd-FLOOR CEILING FRAME
(UNDERSIDE)

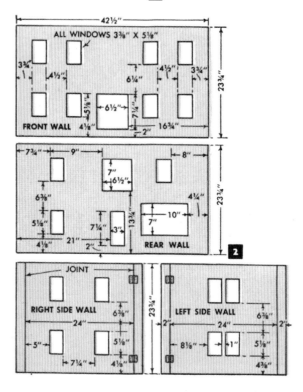

PLANS FOR THE EXTERIOR WALLS

this frame are covered after first installing electrical wires for the lights. Heavily insulated lamp cord will do for connecting the sockets, and all wiring is brought to a central terminal in the attic. A toy-train or bell-ringing transformer, which can be mounted in the attic or placed remotely from the house, is used to light 6-volt bulbs. Use a well insulated, rubber covered extension cord from the 110-volt line to the transformer. A toggle switch to control the transformer is mounted in a corner of the bathroom ceiling. The switch should be wired into the extension cord ahead of the transformer. Be sure that all connections are soldered and taped and that are fixtures and electrical components are UL-rated. Realistic light fixtures can be made by cutting off the base of 7½-watt frosted bulbs and using the top parts as globes. Or an indirect lighting effect can be created by covering the hole for the bulb with a piece of frosted glass and mounting the bulb behind it. The ceiling frame for the second floor, *Fig. 6,* is shown

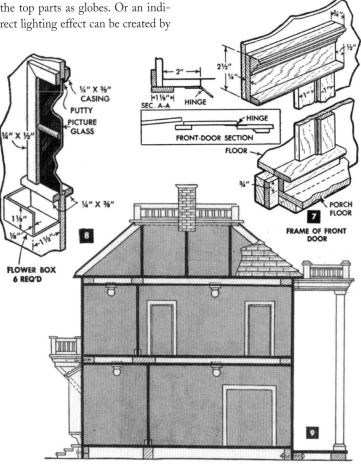

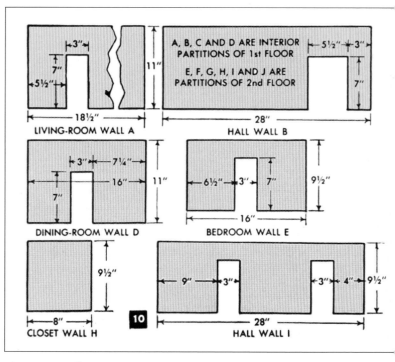

A, B, C AND D ARE INTERIOR
PARTITIONS OF 1st FLOOR

E, F, G, H, I AND J ARE
PARTITIONS OF 2nd FLOOR

LIVING-ROOM WALL A

HALL WALL B

DINING-ROOM WALL D

BEDROOM WALL E

CLOSET WALL H

10

HALL WALL I

PLANS FOR INTERIOR WALLS AND PARTITIONS

ceiling-side up. Note that the partition grooves must be spaced to match those in the top side of the second-floor frame. The top of the ceiling frame is covered with ¼-in. plywood, letting it project 1⅜ in. all around. Remember to include wiring here for second-floor lights.

Cut the partitions, as in *Fig. 10,* next. Note that these are keyed with the floor plans to show where each one goes. The waste pieces from the door openings are saved and used as doors. These can be hinged to actually swing, or they can be left ajar in a fixed position. Interior casing and baseboard are ½-in. strips of cigar-box wood. Let the casing on one side of each opening extend ⅛ in. to form stops for the door, and insert a fill-in

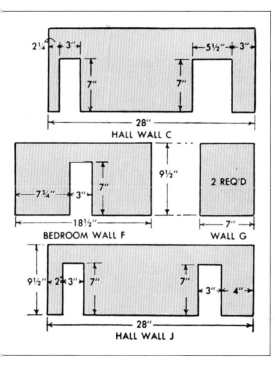

2¼" 3" 5½" 3"
7" 7"
28"
HALL WALL C

9½" 2 REQ'D
7"
7¾" 3"
18½" 7"
BEDROOM WALL F WALL G

9½" 2 3" 7" 7" 3" 4"
28"
HALL WALL J

this time, too. A piece of plywood, 10 in. square and having the edges beveled 45 degrees, is fitted in a corner of the living room as indicated in the first-floor plan. An opening is cut in it first for a fire pit and then the lower half is faced with a mantel, the upper half with a mirror.

Exterior walls are dimensioned in *Fig. 2*. These are also of ¼-in. plywood. The front and rear walls are fastened to the edge of the frames with flat-headed screws, letting them extend ¼ in. at each end and butting the top edge of the plywood against the roof overhang. A 2-in. strip is added to each corner, to which the side walls are hinged. Then each corner is finished with corner boards. See the sectional view to the right of *Fig. 5*. Small turn buttons can be used to keep the sidewalls closed. All windows are trimmed, inside and out, according to *Fig. 8*. The front door is framed,

piece in the exposed groove. It will be somewhat more convenient to decorate the interior if the partitions are painted or papered before they are glued in place. The open stairway in *Fig. 15* must be installed as you go. This fits against wall *C* and requires cutting away a portion of a cross member in the second-floor framing to make it fit flush. The fireplace in *Fig. 14* should be installed at

as in *Fig. 7.* Shutters are added to the second-floor windows.

The hip roof is framed next. A 14-by-27-in. beveled frame is supported 6½ in. above the plywood attic floor by ¾-in. rafters and is roofed with plywood, as in *Fig. 12.* Shingles can be made of cardboard or wood, laid individually or in strips. Finally, the center of the roof is covered with a removable panel as shown, the railing fitted and the two chimneys added. Red paper ruled in a brick pattern with white ink can be pasted to the

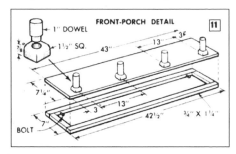

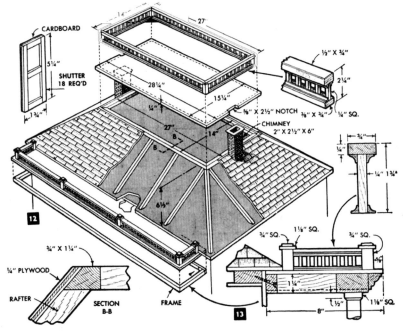

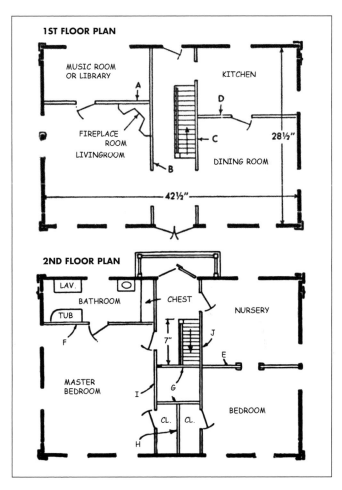

four sides of the chimney. Shingles likewise can be cut from colored cardboard, or painted later to suit. By first coating the shingled roof with a thin application of glue and then sprinkling fine sand on it when the glue is tacky, you can simulate real shingles. Where the shingles

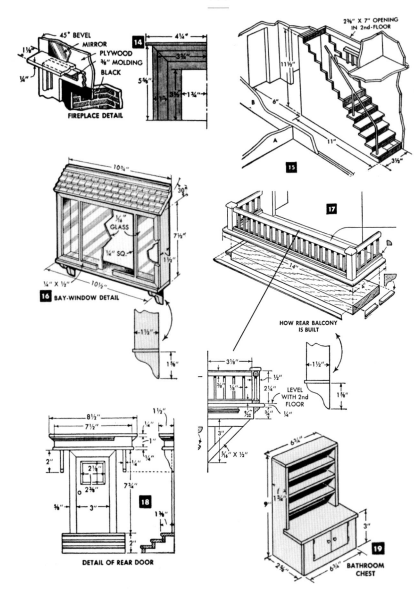

FIREPLACE DETAIL

45° BEVEL
MIRROR
PLYWOOD
3/8" MOLDING
BLACK
1 1/4"
1/4"

14
4 1/4"
3 3/4"
5 5/8"
4 1/4"
3 1/2"
1 3/4"

15
2 3/8" X 7" OPENING IN 2nd-FLOOR
11 1/2"
B
6"
A
11"
3 1/2"

16 **BAY-WINDOW DETAIL**
10 3/4"
30°
1/8" GLASS
1/4" SQ.
7 1/2"
1 1/2"
1/4" X 1/2"
10 1/2"
1 1/2"
1 3/4"

17
HOW REAR BALCONY IS BUILT
14"
1 1/2"
LEVEL WITH 2nd FLOOR
1 1/2"
3 1/8"
1/2"
3/8"
1/8"
2 1/4"
9/32"
3/4"
1/4"
3"
3/4" X 1/2"

18
DETAIL OF REAR DOOR
8 1/2"
7 1/2"
1 1/2"
1/4"
1"
1/4"
1/4"
2"
2 1/4"
2 3/8"
7 3/4"
5/8"
3"
1 3/4"
2"

19 **BATHROOM CHEST**
6 3/4"
1 3/4"
9"
3"
2 3/8"
6 3/4"

THE REAR VIEW OF THE HOUSE

meet at the hip line, cover the joint with a strip of cardboard folded in the center, as shown.

Figs. 11 and *13* detail the porch, and *Fig. 9* shows how the porch floor is bolted to the house. This leaves the balcony, bay window and stoop to be added to the rear side of the house. These are detailed in *Figs. 16, 17,* and *18.* The bathroom chest in *Fig. 19* is located according to the second-floor plan.

— A DOLLHOUSE TURNTABLE —

Playing with a dollhouse can be a lot more fun for a little girl if she has this turntable on which the house can sit. It's at the right height for play and can be turned as she likes without fear of scratching floors or a good table. Fir plywood is used for both the table-top and the rotating turntable. The

tabletop should be made from ¾-in. plywood, while the turntable is best cut out of ½-in. material. Dimensions may be varied to suit the dollhouse. The frame is made of 1⅜-in. pine. Miter the corners as indicated in the detail and drill holes for the screws. Finally, assemble it with wood screws and glue.

The legs are cut from 1⅛-in. pine. Notch the top end to fit into the corners and to overlap the frame, as shown in the detail. Chamfer the bottoms of the legs so that they will not split while in use. Then join the legs to

the underframe with wood screws and glue. The center disk and the bearing ring of the turntable are cut from ¼-in. birch plywood, and attached to the tabletop with glue brads.

The turntable is framed with ½-by-½-in. pine. The hole in the center of both the table and the turntable is ⅜ in. counterbored to take a ⅜-by-2-in. stove bolt. To finish, paint all surfaces with dark-brown semi-gloss oil paint. Coat the top surface of the center disk and the ring bearing with paraffin for smooth turning.

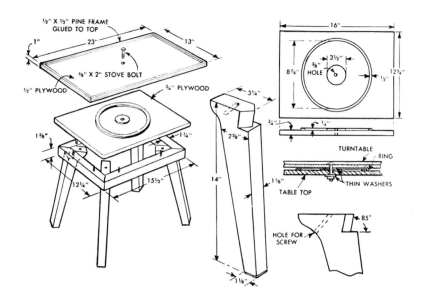

— Apartment Dollhouse Modernized with Elevator —

A sleek modern dollhouse is the perfect project for a modern family to tackle. The four-story, step-back construction of this pressed-wood or plywood dollhouse gives it more room than the average

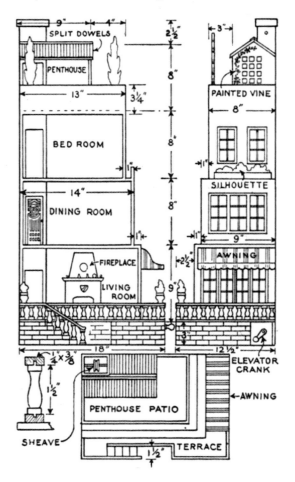

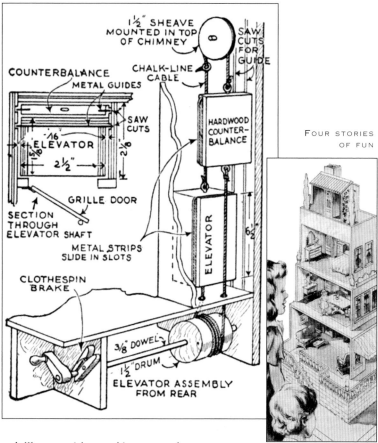

1½" SHEAVE
MOUNTED IN TOP
OF CHIMNEY

SAW
CUTS
FOR
GUIDE

CHALK-LINE
CABLE

COUNTERBALANCE

METAL GUIDES

SAW
CUTS

ELEVATOR

2½"

HARDWOOD
COUNTER-
BALANCE

FOUR STORIES
OF FUN

GRILLE DOOR

SECTION
THROUGH
ELEVATOR SHAFT

METAL STRIPS
SLIDE IN SLOTS

ELEVATOR

6½"

CLOTHESPIN
BRAKE

3/8" DOWEL

1½" DRUM

ELEVATOR ASSEMBLY
FROM REAR

dollhouse, without taking as much floor space. One side of each room is open and only one wall of each room is provided with windows. The elevator shaft is incorporated with the chimney and has a door on each floor. A crank projecting from the basement wall operates the elevator, which remains at any floor by the braking action of a clothespin on the axle. A balustrade around the terrace and a tin awning add to the appearance.

— A NOVEL DOLLHOUSE —

Two little girls abandoned an elaborate dollhouse for the table arrangement shown in the photo. They objected to the ceilings of the other house, which hampered them in moving their dolls and furniture about. One of them conceived the idea of having the rooms partitioned off with railings on top of a table. Later, a taller table for an upper floor was added. Openings are left in the partitions to serve as doorways between the rooms. The two tables are made of light pine, so that they can be easily moved about. Being separate, they can form either a two-story house as shown, or they can be placed end to end to make one long building. The upstairs partitions are higher than those on the lower table, because there they do not interfere with the child's reaching into the different rooms. The furniture is painted in some contrasting color. Most of the toy furniture was made with the help of grown-ups. The front of the lower table is cut out so that a stool may be used while playing. This house has been the most absorbing and useful toy these children have ever owned.

AN OPEN DOLLHOUSE ALLOWS FOR UNRESTRICTED PLAY

— YOU CAN BUILD THIS DOLLHOUSE OF PLYWOOD —

Just think of the pleasure a girl will get from this modern dollhouse! Up-to-the minute styling makes it easy to build, for simplicity is always a feature of modern design. A jigsaw comes in handy for cutting the curved parts, but for the balance you can get along nicely with hand tools and glue.

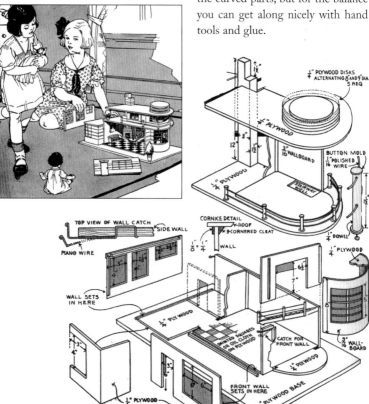

FIG. 1

Practically the whole thing is made of plywood and wallboard. Windows are of transparent celluloid that can be found in art stores. Two walls are made so that they can be lifted out to give easy access to the interior. Plan views are given in *Figs. 1* and *2* a perspective shows the assembly in *Fig. 3*. Only general dimensions are given, this being done so that you

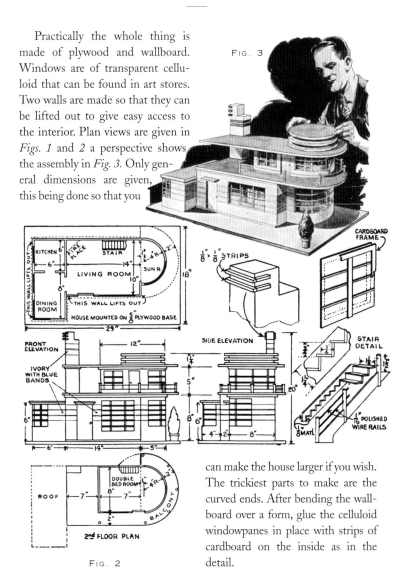

FIG. 3

KITCHEN
FIRE PLACE
STAIR
SUN R.
LIVING ROOM
THIS WALL LIFTS OUT
DINING ROOM
THIS WALL LIFTS OUT
HOUSE MOUNTED ON ⅝ PLYWOOD BASE
6"
14"
18"
10"
6"
8"
29"

⅛" × ⅛" STRIPS

CARDBOARD FRAME

FRONT ELEVATION
IVORY WITH BLUE BANDS
12"
5"
8"
6"
6"
14"
5"

SIDE ELEVATION
20"
6"
4" 2" 8"
⅛ MATL.

STAIR DETAIL
¼" POLISHED WIRE RAILS

ROOF
DOUBLE BED ROOM
7"
8"
7"
2"
BALCONY
2nd FLOOR PLAN

FIG. 2

can make the house larger if you wish. The trickiest parts to make are the curved ends. After bending the wallboard over a form, glue the celluloid windowpanes in place with strips of cardboard on the inside as in the detail.

TINY FINE FURNISHINGS

— FURNISHING THE DOLLHOUSE —

Furniture is what makes a dollhouse really fun. Any girl will be fascinated to follow along—and help as she can—with the process of making these highly detailed pieces. This dollhouse furniture is also simple and sturdy, to stand some pretty rough handling by little girls.

THE LIVING ROOM

Fig. 1 shows the doll's living room furnished with an overstuffed davenport, easy chair, piano, a Governor Winthrop–type of desk, and other suitable pieces. Size and

construction of these pieces are given in *Fig. 2*. The davenport and the easy chair are made up of blocks assembled with brads and casein or white glue. Before assembling the pieces, the sharp corners are rounded off, the upholstery is put on, and the feet are screwed in place. The latter are button molds. Cloth or imitation leather used for upholstering is merely glued onto the wood before the feet are attached. Seams on the edges are covered with upholstery tape also glued in place.

The living room

1

No tacks are required. When cutting the cushion blocks, be sure that they are small enough so that after the upholstery has been applied, they will fit on the seat. The base, pedestal and top of the round-top coffee table are assembled with glue on the raw wood before staining. The tiny feet on this piece are small, whittled knobs.

The Governor Winthrop desk is made up of two blocks glued together. A piece of Bristol board

upon which rows of books have been painted or drawn gives a striking effect if covered with celluloid or cellophane to represent glass. Then scroll-sawed doors are applied. Tapered legs are fastened with glue and brads and the drawer fronts are dummies, the knobs being brass escutcheon pins with the heads pounded square. A strip of wood molding around the base completes the job. It is finished in a mahogany stain and waxed.

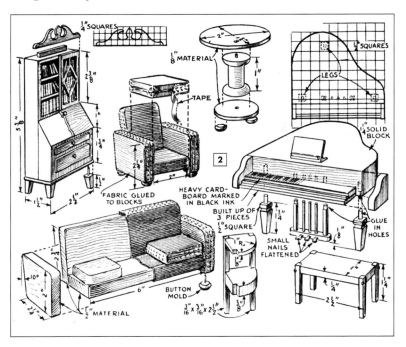

3 Empire style in the dining room

A simple corner table, also included in *Fig. 2*, can be placed in a corner of the room, or two of them set on each side of the davenport. Corners are rabbeted for legs, which are glued in place. It is wise to make the rabbets in the square pieces first and then cut the curve. One of the easiest pieces to make is the grand piano. The box is scroll-sawed from a single block of wood and the keyboard is built up, the keys being marked on Bristol board with a ruling pen. The music rack is glued to the top. Legs are tapered from square stock and fitted with dowels. Pedals are merely brads pounded flat. A piano bench consists of a seat with rabbeted corners for the legs.

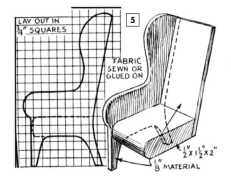

LAY OUT IN ¼" SQUARES

5

FABRIC SEWN OR GLUED ON

½" x 1½" x 2"

⅛" MATERIAL

Another good piece for the living room is the wing chair detailed in *Fig. 5.* Thin material is used for the sides and back, while a thicker piece forms the seat. This piece is not painted, except for the legs, as it is to be covered with fabric. The covering is slipped over the chair, with finishing stitches at the curve of the wings, etc., which gives a trim effect.

EMPIRE STYLE IN THE DINING ROOM

Next comes the dining-room furniture for which Empire Style is shown in *Figs. 3* and *4.* The sideboard is a block of wood with rabbets for the tapered legs, which are glued in place. Drawer fronts are thin material glued on as shown with squared escutcheon-pin heads for

drawer pulls. You will find the oval dining table attractive. Its top is a piece of ¼-in. stock with molded edge. A small screw is inserted up through a hole in the top of the pedestal. In making the pedestal, the bottom is slotted while the stock is square, before turning. Legs are in three pieces: a double one extending through one slot and two single ones glued in the other slots. Each dining chair consists merely of a substantial seat to which the back and the front legs are attached with small dowels and glue, the legs being set in rabbets. The latter are tapered and grooved near the top. As thin wood is used for the backs, they can be scroll-sawed four at a time. For added strength, escutcheon pins are driven diagonally through the front legs and the edge of the seat, a pilot hole being drilled first to avoid splitting.

QUAINT COLONIAL BEDROOM STYLING

A four-poster bed is especially attractive for one of the bedrooms. The posts are not turned, but square stock scored with a file is used.

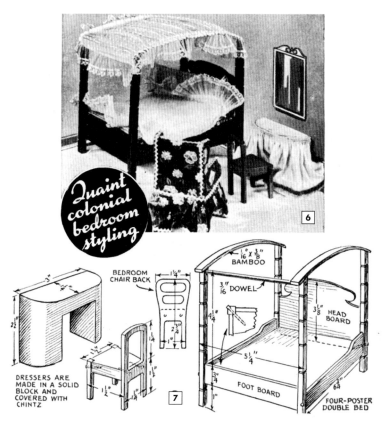

BEDROOM CHAIR BACK

DRESSERS ARE MADE IN A SOLID BLOCK AND COVERED WITH CHINTZ

7

$\frac{1}{16}'' \times \frac{3}{8}''$ BAMBOO

$\frac{3}{16}''$ DOWEL

$3\frac{1}{8}''$ HEAD BOARD

FOOT BOARD

FOUR-POSTER DOUBLE BED

Arched pieces of bamboo, which are heated and bent to shape, span the top to support the covering. See *Figs. 6* and *7*. Bedroom chairs having scroll-sawed backs are in two simple styles. These are made similar to the dining chairs and may be stained or painted white.

THE DOLL CHILD'S ROOM

A dresser is cut out of a single block of wood. The ends are rounded and then a chintz covering is provided. If a mirror is desired, one of appropriate size can be glued to a wood strip. Bunk beds, as in *Figs. 8* and *9*, resemble the full-size pieces except

The doll-child's room

for the actual construction of the bottoms. To assure strength, the bottoms are ½-in. stock, which provides ample surface to which the side members, head- and footboards are glued. The upper unit can be lifted off the lower unit if twin beds are desired. Small dowels in the top of the bedposts of the lower unit prevent the upper one from sliding off. For mattresses, pieces

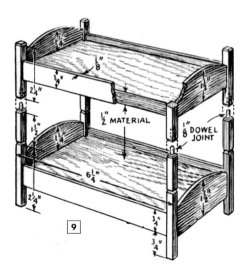

of ⅜-in. wood are used, these being cut to fit loosely in the bed to allow for the "ticking" that is glued on later. Other pieces for the bedrooms, such as a chest of drawers and a linen chest, are cut from blocks of wood in much the same manner as the dining-room side-board. Assembly and sizes of these pieces are given in *Fig. 10.*

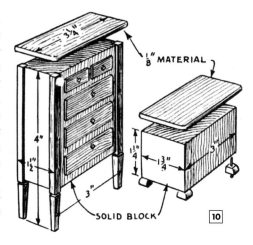

— DOLL CRIB WITH DROP SIDE —

When it comes time for the little girl in your house to put her dolls to bed, she'll love doing it in this crib that is a model of the real thing. Sturdily constructed of plywood set into grooves in a frame of 1-by-1-in. stock, it has a drop side that slides up and down on metal curtain rods secured to the head and foot. Two hardwood turn buttons operated simultaneously by a dowel handle firmly support the drop side in the raised position.

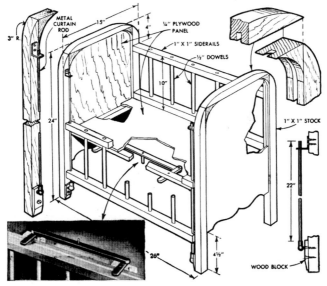

METAL CURTAIN ROD

3" R.

15"

4"

¼" PLYWOOD PANEL

1" X 1" SIDERAILS

½" DOWELS

10"

24"

1" X 1" STOCK

22"

26"

4½"

WOOD BLOCK

THE TWO SIDES ARE IDENTICAL AND ARE MADE BY DRIVING PIECES OF ½-IN. DOWEL THROUGH TWO RAILS MADE OF 1-BY-1-IN. STOCK. SCRAP OF WOOD HOLDS RAILS APART.

— DOLL BED FROM A CIGAR BOX —

A doll bed that any little girl will appreciate can be improvised easily from a cigar box, four empty thread spools and four clothespins. The spools are glued to the corners of the box to form the legs and the clothespins are slipped over the box edges and glued in place to form the posters over which a canopy then can be spread.

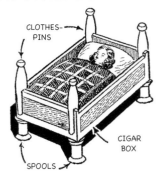

CLOTHES-PINS

CIGAR BOX

SPOOLS

— CARDBOARD DOLL FURNITURE —

Lack of tools or inability to buy thin wood need not discourage you from making doll furniture for the tiny lady member of your family. You can make strong, neat pieces from corrugated cardboard, which can be

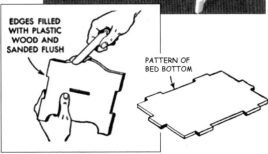

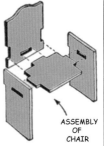

ASSEMBLY OF CHAIR

EDGES FILLED WITH PLASTIC WOOD AND SANDED FLUSH

PATTERN OF BED BOTTOM

cut with a sharp knife and reinforced with wood plastic or other crack filler. The doll bed shown is a good example of what can be done. After cutting the parts to shape and size, fill the edges of each piece with wood plastic to a depth of about ¼ in., allow it to dry and then sand smooth.

This makes the cardboard quite stiff yet springy enough to take a lot of abuse. Mortising and tenoning the parts and gluing all joints adds rigidity. Finish the furniture with paint. The first coat likely will be completely absorbed and, therefore, three coats will be necessary.

ACCESSORIES *in* MINIATURE

— SIMPLE CART FOR DOLL RIDES —

A delight to the heart of very young girls, this pull toy is made with odds and ends that are found in most workshops. The body of the wagon is a small basket that is woven of gaily colored materials. It can be reed, raffia, wicker, or any other suitable material. Place the basket on a piece of plywood and trace the outline on the board. When cutting the base make it about ¾ in. oversize. Next cut the axle and allow it to overlap the base slightly. A length of sturdy dowel is cut to serve as a handle, with a smaller dowel to serve as a crosspiece. Two corner irons are screwed to the wooden axle and roller-skate wheels are bolted to

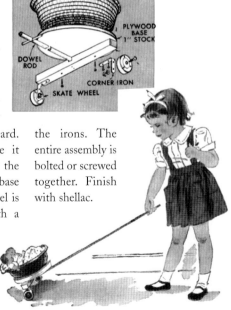

the irons. The entire assembly is bolted or screwed together. Finish with shellac.

— WOODEN DOLL CARRIAGE —

Of much simpler construction than the usual doll carriage, this stroller is easy to make. The wood comes from old boxes and odd pieces of leftover lumber. There is a steering handle for the doll, but it's just for looks and is set into a blind hole in the front axle, which is screwed rigidly in place. For a handle to push the carriage, a length of dowel fits into a block attached to the back, as shown in the circular inset. The wooden wheels turn on long wood screws and spacers between them and the axles keep the rear ones from rubbing against the side.

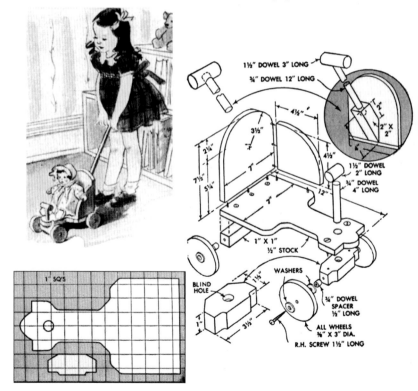

— DOLL SEESAW —

Here's a simple toy that little tots can operate to give dolly a seesaw ride. The chair for the doll can be made to suit, and the rest of the parts proportioned accordingly. Metal shelf brackets pivot the bar on the balancing point.

— STROLLER FOR DOLLY —

Here's a doll buggy that will make the young miss in your family very proud. The buggy is designed to resemble a stroller, and there's no danger of the doll falling out of it as a dowel rod (see detail) keeps her in. A bright enamel finish in contrasting colors like red and blue will decorate and protect the surface of the buggy.

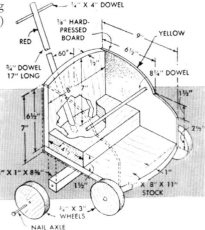

— THE PERFECT DOLL BATH —

This neat little doll bath is easy to make from ½-in. stock, plywood, and rubberized sheeting. The X-frame legs are pivoted at the center to permit folding and the rear tray pivots on a length of dowel that extends through both leg frames. The front end of each tray arm is notched to engage the ends of the towel bar. After the tub pattern is cut from rubberized sheeting, all edges are taped. Then the sheeting is folded, as indicated by the dotted lines, stitched along the taped edges, and hemmed to slip over the rear dowel and the towel bar. The wooden framework and shelf should be painted before assembly.

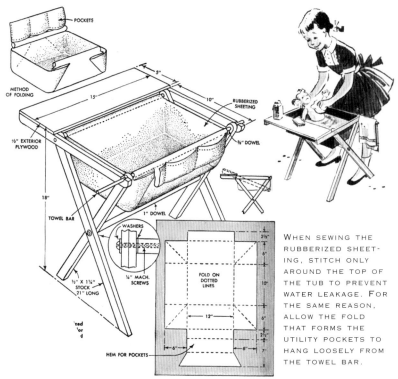

WHEN SEWING THE RUBBERIZED SHEETING, STITCH ONLY AROUND THE TOP OF THE TUB TO PREVENT WATER LEAKAGE. FOR THE SAME REASON, ALLOW THE FOLD THAT FORMS THE UTILITY POCKETS TO HANG LOOSELY FROM THE TOWEL BAR.

{ CHAPTER 3 }

A ROOM
of HER OWN

—

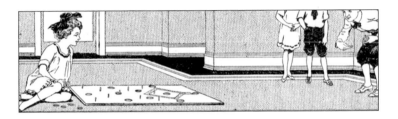

PERFECT PLAYHOUSES

— A WONDERFUL FOLDING PLAYHOUSE —

The child's playhouse is an expensive luxury if it is purchased ready to set up. But by following the instructions given here, families can work together to construct a large and inexpensive model with three walls that fold nearly flat for storage.

Procure about 100 ft. of 1¾ x 1½-in. boards, and saw out the

THE COVERED FRAMEWORK CAN BE USED INDOORS OR OUT.

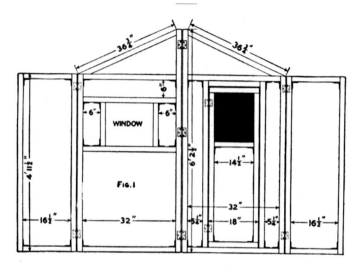

Fig. 1

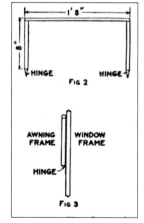

framing pieces, as shown in the diagram. Using iron brackets instead of nails, it will be much easier to construct than if the corners were mortised and nailed or glued.

When the frame is complete, tack burlap or grass cloth over the frame to make the wall covering. Either can be purchased fairly cheaply, and the best color to use is green, red or brown. This material should be fastened onto the different sections before they are hinged together. To prevent the fabric from unraveling, turn the edges under before tacking them down.

A piece of wire screen is used for the door. An old piece will do, if it is well coated with black or dark green pain. It is then tacked onto the inside of the door. Fasten the different parts together with the hinges. The hinges are fastened on the inside of the side wings, and on the outside of the two front pieces. With the hinges placed in this manner, the house can be folded into a very small space indeed.

For one recently built, green burlap was used on the walls, and the door and window frames were trimmed in bright white for a very pretty effect. A small awning was made for over the window, which improved the appearance even more. Roller shades on the door and window, and an electric doorbell, complete a very neat and practical playhouse.

— WEATHERPROOF PLAYHOUSE OF PAINTED WALLBOARD —

An outdoor playhouse is a great fair weather fun structure and can be quickly and easily built of with any of the various types of exterior wallboard such as plywood. Properly painted, especially at the edges, this material will effectively withstand exposure to the weather. The construction and painting is not so difficult that the girl herself can't help out.

Fig. 1 shows an adaptation of an English cottage having a floor space of 10 by 12 ft. For the foundation, lay three parallel sills on flat stones, brick or concrete piers, and nail floor joists to them, spaced 18 in. on centers. Lay a floor of matched boards over the joists and then proceed with the wall frames. Corner construction is shown in *Fig. 3*. The studs can be spaced about 24 in. on center. Allow for door and window openings of sizes given in the elevation drawings, *Fig. 6*. The distance from the floor to the top of the plate, or horizontal piece across the tops of the studs, is 5 ft. The peak of the main roof is 5 ft. above the plate. The smaller roof is 4 ft. above the plate. Spacing of the rafters depends on the kind of wallboard used for sheathing. Light wallboard will require rafters fairly close together, while a heavy, stiff wallboard such as plywood will allow greater spacing. Curved strips are nailed to the rafters and cornice over the tiny porch. After the framework

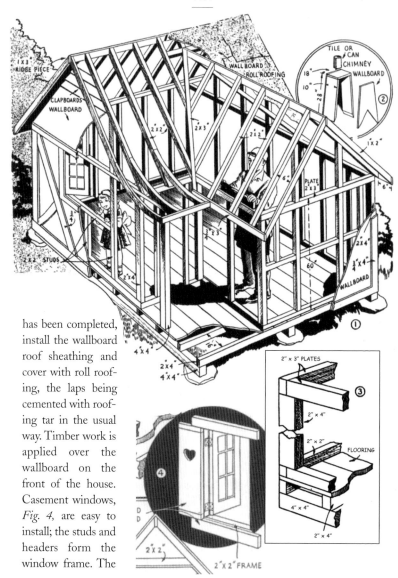

has been completed, install the wallboard roof sheathing and cover with roll roofing, the laps being cemented with roofing tar in the usual way. Timber work is applied over the wallboard on the front of the house. Casement windows, *Fig. 4,* are easy to install; the studs and headers form the window frame. The

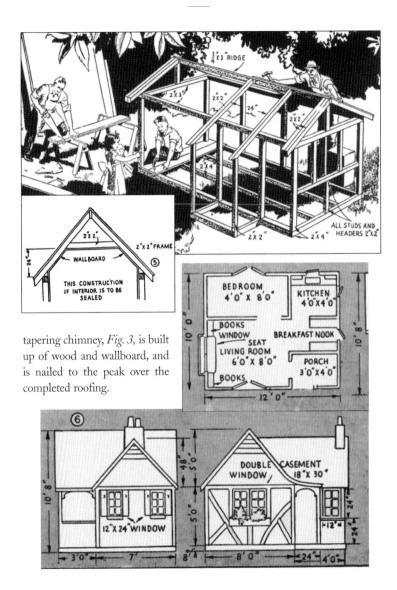

tapering chimney, *Fig. 3,* is built up of wood and wallboard, and is nailed to the peak over the completed roofing.

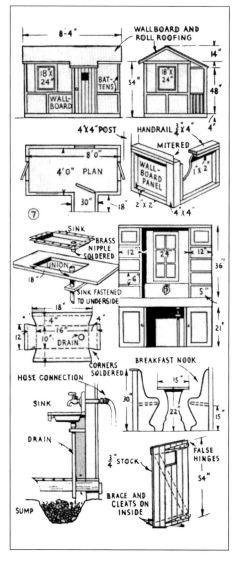

Of course, sealing the inside and trimming with battens will greatly improve the appearance of the interior. In this case, crosspieces should join the rafters horizontally about 2 ft. above the eaves as shown in *Fig. 5*. It is important that the wallboard be painted on the outside to prevent it from absorbing moisture, and it is wise to give the inside one coat also, if the house is to be exposed to continued wet weather. In any case, paint the walls before applying the timber work and molding so that they will not become daubed in the course of painting.

A kitchen sink with a drain and running water can easily be made, as in *Fig. 7*. The tap is screwed onto a short length of pipe extending outside the wall, which is coupled to the garden hose. From a sheet of galvanized iron, cut the sink according to the pattern given, bending on the dotted lines and soldering the corners. Also solder a short brass or galvanized

THE FINISHED PLAYHOUSE

nipple at the drain hole. The sink is fastened under the opening in the drain board, and the nipple inserted in a union at the top of a ¾-in. galvanized straight pipe. The nipple sets in loosely, and the pipe, passing through the floor, drains into a hole filled with gravel. The breakfast nook is formed by a low partition and is fitted with fixed seats and a movable table. A front door is easily built of matched boards with a small, glazed window, cleats and diagonal brace on the inside, and false strap hinges on the weather side.

A simpler design of playhouse is given in the upper details of *Fig. 7.* Note that the windows in the front and rear walls are fixed, while those in the ends are hinged to swing out for ventilation. The little porch with its spindle rail breaks up the angularity of the house, which is decidedly inviting in spite of its low cost. A suggested color scheme for the house is ivory or white walls, dark oak stain on the door, woodwork, molding, and window frames, with green roof and shutters. The floor can be stained and waxed.

— "PREFAB" PLAY COTTAGE —

There are few toys that delight a little girl like a walk-in playhouse. This plywood cottage is a yard toy that will bring many hours of pleasure and it is small enough for indoor use in rainy weather or during the cold months. Designed to be set up or taken down in just a few minutes, the cottage collapses to form a compact unit that can be stored under a bed or in a closet. The sides, roof, and trim are cut from three 4-by-8-ft. sheets of plywood, and a few lengths of solid stock are required for uprights, plates, cleats, and ridge board. Although ⅜-in. plywood was used on the original house, ¼-in. plywood or hardboard will serve the purpose. If the house is to remain outdoors during the summer months, be sure to use weatherproof (marine-type) plywood for the walls and roof. Note in the details how the corner uprights of the sidepieces are fitted with bolts that engage notches cut in the corner uprights of the end panels. Wing nuts lock the uprights together for quick assembly.

The ridge board is notched to fit over the gables and drilled to receive dowels inserted near the upper edge of each roof panel. Valances and cleats form channels near the ends of the roof panels. The channels engage the edges of the gables. Sills, lintels, and doorway trim are glued and screwed directly to the plywood panels, but the window boxes are given the effect of depth by mounting them on ¾-in.-sq. space blocks fastened to the plywood.

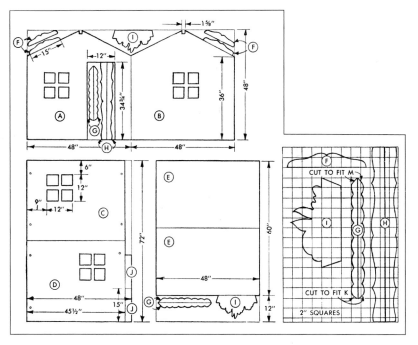

If the house is intended primarily for outdoor use, it will be worthwhile to include a raised floor to keep the children off damp ground. The floor can be made by screwing a sheet of plywood or hardboard to 1-by-2-in. joists set on edge. The joists should be spaced not more than 12 in. apart. To facilitate storage, make the floor in two parts, hinging them together, if desired. Notch the corners of the floor to clear the uprights when the walls are set up around it. The floor can be painted with porch enamel or marine varnish and made even more attractive by covering it with a remnant of linoleum. Paint the walls, roof, and trim of the house in bright colors and, if you wish, hang plastic or oilcloth curtains at the windows. Although a door is not necessary, a simple one can be made by hinging a plywood panel to the doorway, fitting the panel with a knob-type drawer pull on each side. Make sure that the door fits loosely enough so that it will not stick.

Fun Furniture

— A Tea Party Serving Cart —

This serving cart makes tea parties more fun for the tiny hostess and her guests. The upraised arms of jigsawed cutouts hold a scalloped tray. The pull-apart detail above shows how the cart is assembled. Except for

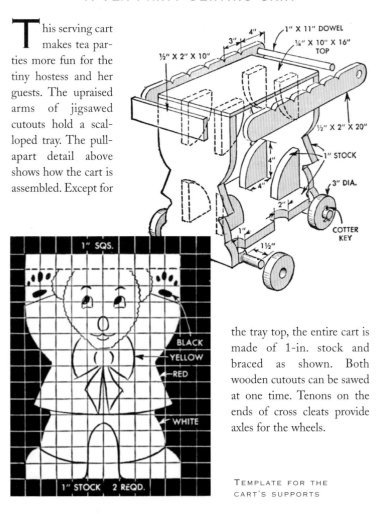

the tray top, the entire cart is made of 1-in. stock and braced as shown. Both wooden cutouts can be sawed at one time. Tenons on the ends of cross cleats provide axles for the wheels.

TEMPLATE FOR THE
CART'S SUPPORTS

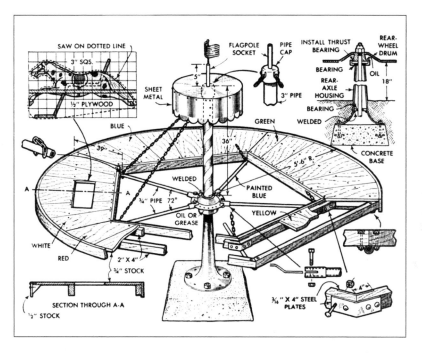

The pedestal-and-spindle assembly on which the merry-go-round turns is the rear axle and housing from a car, cut down and bolted to a concrete base as shown in the detail. The same detail indicates the mounting for the rear-wheel drum. After completing this part of the assembly, weld a 36-in. length of 3-in. pipe to the top of the drum and screw on a pipe cap. Then weld the flagpole socket to the cap. The lengths of pipe that serve as struts to connect the pedestal to the wooden platform are cut and assembled as shown in the center and lower right-hand details. Finally, attach chain braces to the struts and pipe cap, and weld the sheet-metal canopy in place. Seats for the merry-go-round can be of a size and design to suit the age of the children. A pattern for a pinto pony is given, and the photo suggests a few other types. Finish the ride with gaily colored enamels.

— A BACKYARD SLIDE —

Set up in your backyard, this slide will afford a girl and her friends many hours of pleasure, safe from street traffic, and it can be dismantled and stored for the winter in a jiffy. A wide slide bed, stairs, and "take-off plate" all make for safety of the children,

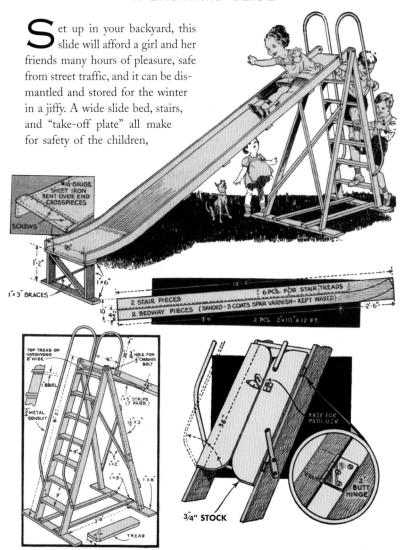

#16-GAUGE
SHEET IRON
BENT OVER END
CROSSPIECES

SCREWS

18"

1'-2"

1"x3" BRACES

1"x6"

10"

4½"

12'-0"

6 PCS. FOR STAIR TREADS

2 STAIR PIECES

2 BEDWAY PIECES (SANDED - 3 COATS SPAR VARNISH - KEPT WAXED)

2'-6"

9'-0"

2 PCS. 2"x10"x12 FT.

TOP TREAD OF
HARDWOOD
6" WIDE

16"

½" HOLE FOR
¾" CARRIAGE
BOLT

1" BEVEL

1"x3" STRIPS
(7 REQ'D.)

¾" METAL
CONDUIT

1½"x3"

1½"x2"

9"

1"x2"

1"x3"

1"x6"

9"

3'-0"

TREAD

36"

HASP FOR
PADLOCK

2"
BUTT
HINGE

¾" STOCK

and a couple of hinged boards near the bottom of the stairs can be locked over the bed to keep tiny tots from climbing the slide without supervision. A sheet-iron bed assures long life, and hardwood bed pieces well sanded and varnished reduce the splinter hazard to a minimum.

— "Skip Scotch" Beach Game —

Requiring only a floating court and two sets of wooden disks, all of which can be made in a few hours, "skip scotch" is an action-packed game that provides real fun at the beach. After the court has

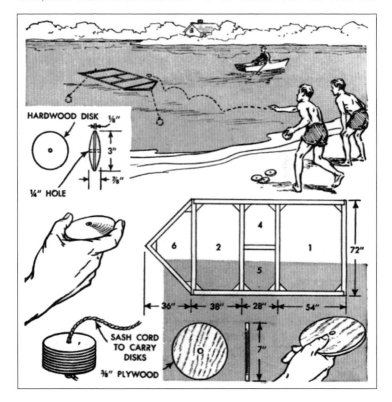

HARDWOOD DISK ⅛"

3"

⅞"

¼" HOLE

SASH CORD TO CARRY DISKS

⅜" PLYWOOD

36" 38" 28" 54"

72"

6 2 1

4

5

7"

been anchored in the water 60 ft. from the shoreline, each player attempts to skip four disks into the highest-scoring section of the court. The first player to score 18 points is the winner of the game. The court sections are numbered as shown in the detail, the front, or triangular, section having the highest number of points. One point is subtracted from the player's score for each disk that misses the court, and disks that come to rest on the framework are not counted. These rules, of course, are merely suggested ones and they can be altered as desired. The wooden framework is made as shown and, after the top has been painted white so it can be seen easily, the entire court is given a coat of spar varnish. Small convex disks can be made of hardwood, or larger, flat disks of waterproof plywood can be used. One set of disks is painted yellow and the other set red, all of them being given a final coat of spar varnish. Before painting, the centers of the disks are drilled so they can be strung on a length of sash cord or clothesline for carrying. Anchors attached to the front and rear of the court hold it in position, and their lines should be as short as possible to keep the court from swinging. Cans filled with concrete will provide anchors. If the game is to be carried in a car, the court can be hinged to fold compactly or made in two or more separate sections that can be quickly hooked or screwed together at the beach and later taken apart in a few minutes for carrying.

— How to Make a Venetian Swing —

The Venetian or gondola swing is an old enough feature of amusement in public parks, but it is seldom used in private grounds, although it is not by any means hard to build. It is an ideal yard toy for a little girl and her friends—one that can in time be handed down to younger siblings. Built properly, it will stand any amount of abuse, and the high sides of the gondola, or car, make it safe for the little ones. The design shown in the illustration has, moreover, an interesting feature that makes it a prime favorite with the children. The sides of the gondola have four disks painted to represent faces, the eyes of which roll and the tongues loll from side to side as the car swings.

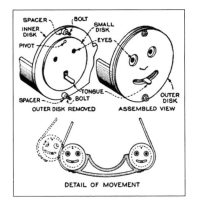

SPACER
BOLT
SMALL DISK
INNER DISK
EYES
PIVOT
TONGUE
SPACER
BOLT
OUTER DISK
OUTER DISK REMOVED
ASSEMBLED VIEW

DETAIL OF MOVEMENT

The construction is simple. A pattern for the sides of the car, which may be of any size desired, is given in the detail drawing. The ends are perfectly circular, and four disks of the same size as the ends are cut at the same time, from the same material. Four smaller disks, about 3 or 4 in. less in diameter, may also be cut. A large disk is fitted to each end, as shown, by means of bolts, with spacers slipped over them so as to leave room for the smaller disks to

WHEN THE SWING IS OPERATED, THE EYES ON ITS SIDES ROLL AND THE TONGUES LOLL FROM SIDE TO SIDE IN A REALISTIC MANNER.

UPPER LEFT: PATTERN OF SIDES.
UPPER RIGHT: DETAIL OF SUSPENSION.
CENTER: ASSEMBLY DRAWING, SHOWING FRAME CONSTRUCTION.
RIGHT: METHOD OF FASTENING SUSPENSION RODS TO
CONNECTING-ROD END.

work between. The outer disks may then be laid aside, the smaller ones centered on the ends of the car sides, and pivoted to them, either with heavy screws or with bolts. After this the position of the tongues may be marked on them. Two holes for the eyes are then bored in each of the larger disks, the location and length of the tongue slots or mouths marked, and the disks slotted.

The tongues are simply strips of flat iron, bent and screwed to the inner disks and painted red. The eyes on the disks are merely large black dots. When the swing is operated, the inner disks swing from side to side, the length of the swing being governed by the length of the mouth slots.

The car is suspended by four ⅜ or ½-in. iron rods. These are flattened at the bottom, bent to conform to the shape of the car, and screwed in place. They are also flattened at the top, bent, drilled, and bolted to the cut-off ends of two old auto-engine connecting rods. These are mounted on a shaft of proper size, secured by means of eyebolts to the crossbar of the swing frame. Collars should be provided at each end of the shaft and on either side of the connecting rods, to prevent endwise motion.

The frame needs no description, but the method of operating the swing may perhaps be new to many. The top board of the frame cross-member is made as wide and as stout as possible, and from it two ropes are hung, in the center, reaching down to the car. The ropes are crossed, and the occupants off the seats, by pulling the ropes alternately, set it in motion and keep it going. Of course, the farther apart the ropes are at the top, the easier it is to start and operate the swing. So an additional length of 2-by-4-in. lumber may be bolted at right angles to the upper frame cross member, as indicated by the dotted lines in the detail, and the ropes attached to the ends of this.

BIG BASEMENT PASTIMES

— BASEMENT GOLF —

Popularity of miniature golf has brought the game right into your basement in the form of a knockdown course that can be picked up and stored away almost as easily as you would a game of croquet. Standard putters and irons are used and scoring is done as in real golf, penalties being counted as strokes. As for space, most basements—especially those with compact heating units—will accommodate the "concentrated" nine-hole course pictured in the illustration. Where there's only a minimum of space, a lot of fun can still be had from a much smaller course. Because each green is complete in itself and lightweight, the course can be set up quickly. Most of the greens are fairly shallow, to permit stacking them in a confined space when not in use.

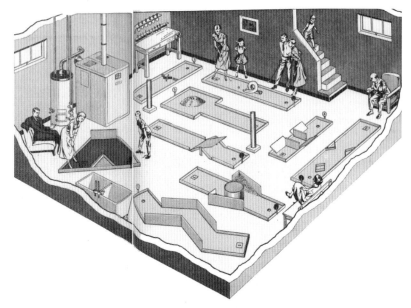

HERE IS A TYPICAL LAYOUT THAT REQUIRES SPACE NO LARGER THAN 14 BY 16 FT. FOR USE IN AN AVERAGE-SIZE BASEMENT. ACTUAL LAYOUT DEPENDS ON THE SHAPE OF THE BASEMENT.

Where yard area is sufficient to permit an outdoor course, a suggested layout for an 18-hole one is given in the plan view. Construction of nine additional greens is given to supplement the nine shown.

The various greens detailed can be adapted to almost any size layout. Though the ones shown have been purposely kept small, the fairways being only 24 in. wide, they can be made larger if space permits, and made even more tricky. In laying out your course, remember to place the greens in numerical order, keeping the tee of the following green adjacent to the hole of the preceding green. The last hole, whether it is No. 9 or 18 of the course, should be located so that the player is brought back to the starting point. It is wise, too, to place the greens so that the first and last holes are near the basement stairway. In designing your own special greens, don't make a hole-in-one shot impossible. Rather, design and locate the hazard in such a manner that the ball can be banked into the cup. The plan view for the 18-hole course shows by dotted lines how it is possible to make each hole in only one shot.

Figs. 1 to *18* inclusive detail the construction of all 18 greens. Old carpeting tacked to the edges of the framework is perhaps the best material to use for the turf. The basement floor is much too smooth for accurate control of the ball. Jute padding and coco matting can also be used. For an outdoor course, sawdust is rec-

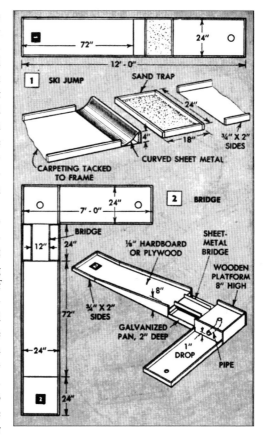

ommended for the playing surface, as in *Fig. 19*. This is spread over a dirt fill to produce a layer about 1 in. deep when the sawdust has been dampened and rolled smooth. Commercial courses generally use a con-

crete base topped with sawdust. If desired, the sawdust can be colored green to look like turf by dyeing it with water-soluble dyes. Shallow can lids are used for cups. *Fig. 20* shows how these are set flush with the rug

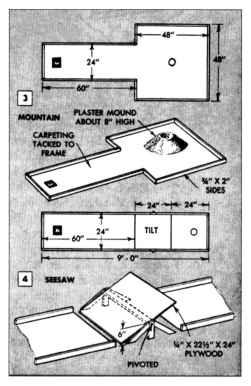

inclined fairway carries the ball over a small bridge. If it misses the bridge, the ball falls into a shallow pan of water with the player being penalized one stroke for lifting it out. The lower end of the pipe that guides the ball to the cup should be in direct line with the cup to permit a hole-in-one shot. The mountain, green No. 3, has the cup placed in the center of a mound of plaster of Paris. The hazard at green No. 4 consists of a plywood panel critically balanced so that the weight of the ball in rolling over it causes the panel to tilt forward toward the cup. In the case of an outdoor course, the hill in green No. 5 can be formed from a mound of dirt, but indoors it is made from sheet metal or linoleum that is bowed and placed across the center of the fairway. An alternate hazard is provided at this hole in the form of a hurdle that is a board set vertically over which a ball must be lifted. For

pile in holes cut in the carpet. Adhesive tape applied across the underside keeps the cups from falling out when the center is glued to each green to serve as a tee. A can-cover marker attached to the far end of the green identifies each hole.

Green No. 1 features a hazard of curved sheet metal to lift the ball over a sand trap. In green No. 2, an

this shot, an iron is provided and left at the hole after play is completed. The maze at green No. 6 is formed from strips of ½-by-1½-in. wood that are tacked in place to the carpeting from the underside.

The obstacle for green No. 7 is made up of short pegs set vertically in front of a sheet-metal bunker. Note that the center space between the pegs must line up with the cup to permit a hole-in-one shot. The pegs can be fastened in position by nailing a wooden strip across the underside of the carpet fairway and then driving screws through the strip and up into the pegs. The strip, cut to fit between the side members, causes a slight hump directly under the pegs. This adds to the difficulty of making a hole-in-one. The pivot point for the turnstile at green No. 8 is placed off center of the fairway so that the blade at the right-hand side is directly in line between the

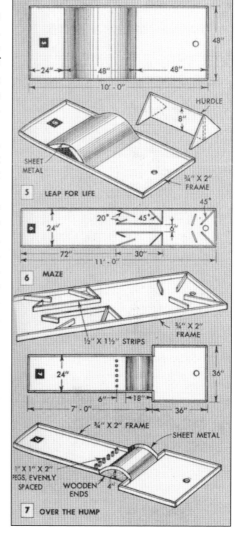

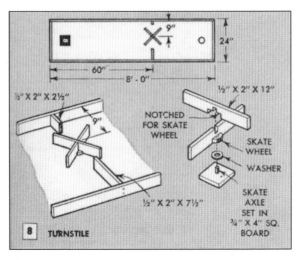

9″

24″

60″

8′ - 0″

½″ X 2″ X 2½″

9″

NOTCHED
FOR SKATE
WHEEL

½″ X 2″ X 12″

SKATE
WHEEL

WASHER

½″ X 2″ X 7½″

SKATE
AXLE
SET IN
¾″ X 4″ SQ.
BOARD

8 TURNSTILE

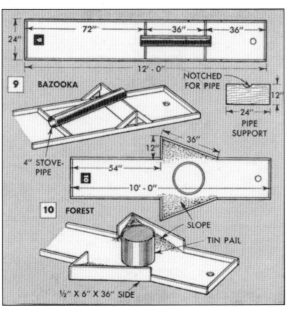

72″

36″

36″

24″

12′ - 0″

9 BAZOOKA

NOTCHED
FOR PIPE

12″

24″

PIPE
SUPPORT

4″ STOVE-
PIPE

36″

12″

54″

10′ - 0″

10 FOREST

SLOPE

TIN PAIL

½″ X 6″ X 36″ SIDE

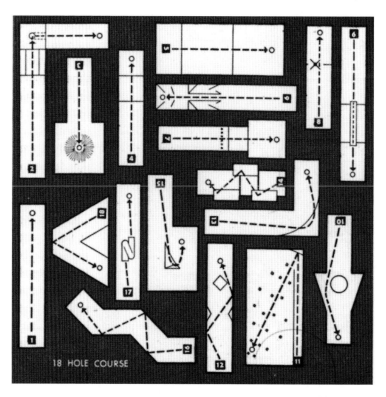

18 HOLE COURSE

tee and the cup. Be sure that the amount of clearance under the turnstile will not allow the ball to roll under it. The bazooka hazard at green No. 9 consists of a length of small stovepipe placed at an angle, the lower end being sunken slightly in the green to permit the ball to enter the pipe easily.

On an outdoor course, green No. 10 is built around a tree, if possible, although a barrel or a 5-gal. pail will serve the same purpose. The fairway is sloped on each side of the tree to bank the ball. Dirt or concrete can be used to form the bank on an outdoor course, while indoors a piece of wood and sheet metal are used as shown in detail *A, Fig. 13*. The pegs at green No. 11 are placed so that a

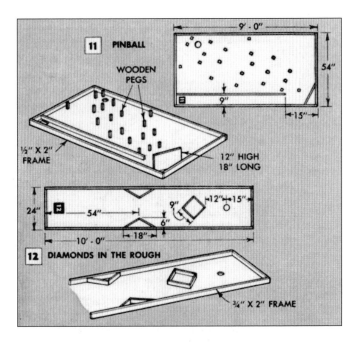

11 PINBALL

WOODEN PEGS

½" X 2" FRAME

12" HIGH
18" LONG

9' - 0"
54"
9"
15"

24"
54"
9"
12"
15"
6"
18"
10' - 0"

12 DIAMONDS IN THE ROUGH

¾" X 2" FRAME

narrow path is kept open between the bank board and the cup. The proper angle to set the bank board so that it directs the ball into the cup is found by experiment. In building this green, the bottom of the framework must be covered with a panel of plywood or hardboard so that the pegs can be attached to it after the carpet is in place. Wooden forms are obstacles along the fairway of green No. 12. L-shaped green No. 13 requires a bank shot to direct the ball to the cup. Overshooting is penalized a stroke.

Green No. 14 requires a trick shot to make the cup. Three inclined boards, staggered opposite each other, and two vertical obstacles placed across the fairway require rolling the ball up over the inclined pieces to get around the two vertical obstacles. Here, cleats fit to the framework to permit nailing the obstacles in place. Green No. 15 requires another bank shot

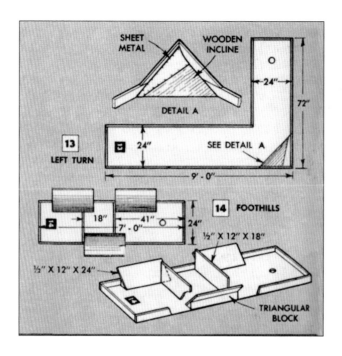

SHEET METAL

WOODEN INCLINE

DETAIL A

24″

72″

13 **LEFT TURN**

24″

SEE DETAIL A

9′ - 0″

14 **FOOTHILLS**

18″   41″   24″

7′ - 0″

½″ X 12″ X 18″

½″ X 12″ X 24″

TRIANGULAR BLOCK

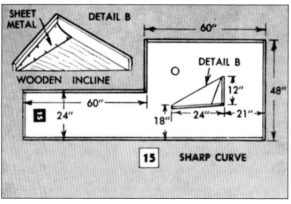

SHEET METAL   **DETAIL B**

60″

DETAIL B

12″

WOODEN INCLINE

60″   18″   24″   21″   48″

24″

15   **SHARP CURVE**

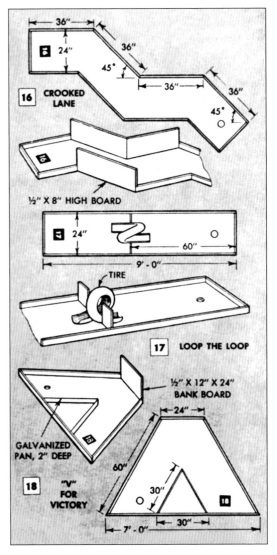

16 CROOKED LANE

36″ · 24″ · 36″ · 45° · 36″ · 36″ · 45°

½″ X 8″ HIGH BOARD

3 24″ · 60″ · 9′ - 0″

TIRE

17 LOOP THE LOOP

½″ X 12″ X 24″ BANK BOARD

GALVANIZED PAN, 2″ DEEP

18 "V" FOR VICTORY

60″ · 24″ · 30″ · 30″ · 7′ - 0″ · 30″

and accurate aim. The incline, detail *B*, is formed from sheet metal and plywood and is located the distance indicated from the cup. This can be fastened directly to the carpet. Green No. 16 requires a triple-bank shot to make a hole-in-one. Bank boards are erected along the side of the fairway at the points indicated.

Sinking a putt on green No. 17 requires the ball to loop through section of old auto tire. The ends of the tire are spread apart as shown, and screwed in the center of the fairway to a base-board nailed to the edges of the framework. Wooden baffles are erected at each side of the tire so that the ball must pass through the tire

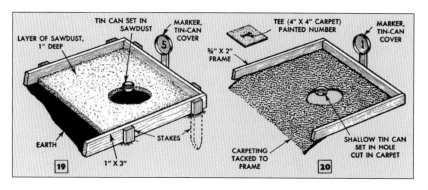

to enter the cup. The fairway of green No. 18 is made V-shaped, with a bank shot being required to sink the putt. A water hazard is installed level with the surface of the fairway. A tri-angular shaped pan of sheet metal 2 in. deep is made to set down into the green. This requires making the frame members wider than actually shown to permit raising the fairway.

— SMALL ROPE USED AS MARBLE RING TO PLAY GAME INDOORS —

When the weather will not permit children to play marbles outdoors where a suitable ring can be chalked on the sidewalk, you can provide them with a ring that can be used on the rug or linoleum. Simply join the ends of a length of cotton clothesline with a piece of adhesive tape. Marbles may be considered "out" when they strike the rope, or the game may be made more difficult by obliging the players to

knock them over the barrier in order to score.

— THROW BEAN BAGS FOR FUN —

This indoor game looks easy at first sight, but when you try it you'll find it's a game of skill that will hold you for hours at a time. It's something like pitching horseshoes

except that the score is made—or lost—by tossing small beanbags through holes cut in a vertical panel. The winning number of points may be decided upon by the opposing teams and the score of the individual players recorded on the scoreboard provided.

After passing through the holes in the panel, the bags slide down to the bottom and collect behind a rectangular opening from which they are easily removed. Note that when the box is set up, the weight rests on the "feet" cut in the lower end of the panel and on the braces. The latter are of a length to tilt the box back slightly so that it stands firmly. The cloth bags, four for each player, measure about 3½ by 5 in. and are filled about three-fourths full of dry beans or clean pebbles of uniform size.

— MARBLE "CROQUET" IS

AN INTERESTING INDOOR GAME

This novel marble game can be played on any flat surface, such as a floor or table-top. The game is somewhat like croquet, the object being to shoot a marble through eight cardboard wickets, the winner is the one who accomplishes this in the least number of plays. The wickets are pieces of cardboard hinged together with tape as indicated. Each wicket has a centralized hole at the lower side, trian-

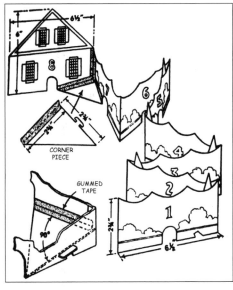

gular pieces of cardboard being used to keep the marbles from lodging in the corners where the wickets are hinged together. Each piece is set in at a slight angle and is hinged to one of the wickets. A tab fits into a slot in the opposite wicket to lock the piece in place and help make the wicket assembly rigid. When not in use, the assembly folds flat for storage. Rules of the game are varied. One shot in turn is the prevailing rule. If an opponent's play causes your marble to pass through a hole, your position is advanced or penalized, accordingly, and your next play is resumed from that point.

— THE RACING GREYHOUNDS —

Here is a fascinating party game that consists of an inclined board having a number of tracks in which miniature greyhounds are sent scooting along in a rather erratic and uncertain way, as shown in *Figs. 1* and *2*. The motive force is supplied by a small motor-driven paddle wheel, which bats golf balls with varying force against the

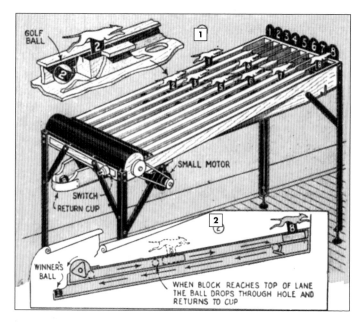

GOLF BALL

SMALL MOTOR

SWITCH

RETURN CUP

WINNER'S BALL

WHEN BLOCK REACHES TOP OF LANE THE BALL DROPS THROUGH HOLE AND RETURNS TO CUP

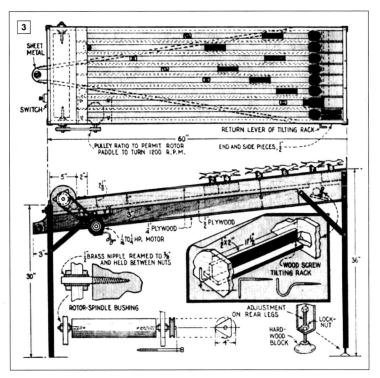

blocks on which the dogs are mounted. By carefully examining the drawings that show the construction details of this game, you will soon get an accurate idea of just how the mechanism works and how the various parts are assembled.

Strips of ¼-in. plywood are used to divide the top into eight 2-in. lanes in which the smooth blocks that hold the dogs are placed. The

three-sided paddle wheel at the lower end of the table should be made of hard maple, and should travel at a speed of from 800 to 1,200 r.p.m. Care must be taken to balance the paddle wheel well to prevent undue vibration. Almost any small motor will serve to supply the necessary power, and a snap or toggle switch is placed at a convenient position as shown in the drawing. When play-

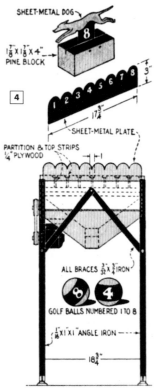

SHEET·METAL DOG

$1\frac{7}{8}" \times 1\frac{7}{8}" \times 4"$ PINE BLOCK

8

4

$\frac{3}{8}"$

1 2 3 4 5 6 7 8

$17\frac{3}{4}"$

SHEET·METAL PLATE

PARTITION & TOP STRIPS $\frac{1}{4}"$ PLYWOOD

1

ALL BRACES $\frac{3}{4}" \times \frac{3}{4}"$ IRON

8 4

GOLF BALLS NUMBERED 1 TO 8

$\frac{1}{8}" \times 1" \times 1"$ ANGLE IRON

$18\frac{3}{4}"$

ing the game, the first dog that reaches the upper end of the track wins the race. The ball that has been striking it, and is correspondingly numbered, then falls through a hole at the end of the track, into a return trough that leads to a cup just below the starting point. The frame for the table and the return trough are shown in *Fig. 5*. Each track, of course, has a hole at its upper end, and in order to prevent any other ball than the winner's from getting into the return trough, a wooden stop is placed directly underneath the row of holes. The stop consists of two pieces of ¼-in. plywood assembled as shown in a detail of *Figs. 3* and *4*, and pivoted at each end. As soon as a ball drops on the horizontal part, the stop moves over to close the row of holes, preventing any more balls from entering. When a race is finished the motor is turned off, the dogs are all

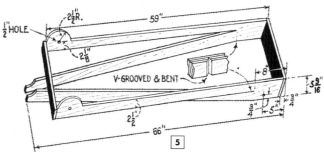

$2\frac{1}{2}"$R.

$\frac{1}{2}"$ HOLE

59"

$2\frac{1}{8}"$

V-GROOVED & BENT

8"

$5\frac{9}{16}"$

$2\frac{1}{2}"$

$\frac{3}{4}"$ 5" $\frac{3}{4}"$

66"

5

pulled down to the starting position with the balls behind them, the stop is moved over to open the holes and the motor is turned on again for the next race.

It is best to enclose the paddle wheel in a sheet-metal shield. Also, it is convenient to make the legs collapsible, and therefore, angle iron may be used to advantage, rigidity being obtained by means of flat-iron corner braces.

GOOD TIMES *on the* TABLETOP

— HANDY GAME BOARD —

A game board can be set right into the driveway by setting tiles cut to the proper shape in the concrete while it is wet. Then the numbers are painted on the tiles with white paint. Although in this case the tiles were set in cement, the entire game could also be painted on a driveway.

— "SWING BALL" —

"Bowling" on a tabletop requires skill, provides plenty of action, and gives the entire family wholesome diversion on long, winter evenings. You count strikes and spares, as in regular bowling, but you play with a suspended ball, manipulation of which requires some of the precision of billiards. The pins are turned on a lathe and the game board is arranged to fold compactly, forming a box in which all the loose parts can be stored. Or, if desired, a game board that is portable, but not folding, can be provided.

The ten pins and their arrangement is similar to the conventional bowling set-up, except that the triangular bank of pins points away from the player instead of facing the player, and is located on one side of the center line. The suspended ball is four times heavier than a single pin and crashes through the bank of pins the same way as a bowling ball does on an alley, after which it returns to the hand of the player. The ball must be swung in an elliptical path, hitting the pins on the return swing. It is this part of the game that gives rise to some interesting calculations. Regardless of which point the

THIS TABLE-BOWLING GAME IN WHICH A SWINGING BALL IS BROUGHT TO BEAR UPON A BANK OF TEN PINS, HAS MANY POINTS IN COMMON WITH THE USUAL BOWLING GAME.

counts the score plus the ten of the strike plus the number of pins made in his next two swings. In the case of a spare, she adds the ten of the spare to the score, plus the number of pins made on her next swing. Two swings—unless a strike is made—constitute a frame, and ten frames make a line, or game. If a pin is knocked over on the forward swing, if a player fails to catch the ball on its return swing, if the pins are missed entirely, or if the ball strikes the leg of the tripod, it is deemed a gutter ball and constitutes a scoreless play in which any pins that may have been knocked over do not count. These will give you some idea of how the game is played. But if you are unacquainted with conventional bowling, it is good idea to visit a local bowling alley or a friend who knows the game so that you can familiarize yourself with the details of scoring. Regular bowling score sheets can be purchased at amusement supply stores, or one can be permanently painted on a chalkboard.

ball begins its course, or how wide the ellipse traveled, the distances *A* and *B*, as shown in *Fig. 7* are always the same.

In the game, you follow rules of conventional bowling. Players alternate, swinging the ball twice at each turn unless all pins are knocked down with the first swing, which is a strike. Knocking all the pins down in two swings gives you a "spare." When a player makes a strike she

The game table is made up of four panels of ¼-in. plywood or hard-pressed board. These panels, laid out in their respective positions, are covered with a piece of 8-oz. canvas that

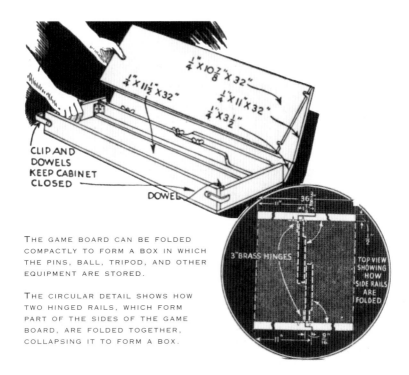

THE GAME BOARD CAN BE FOLDED COMPACTLY TO FORM A BOX IN WHICH THE PINS, BALL, TRIPOD, AND OTHER EQUIPMENT ARE STORED.

THE CIRCULAR DETAIL SHOWS HOW TWO HINGED RAILS, WHICH FORM PART OF THE SIDES OF THE GAME BOARD, ARE FOLDED TOGETHER, COLLAPSING IT TO FORM A BOX.

is glued on. After the glue has set, the surplus cloth at the edges is trimmed away and the end piece and side pieces are mounted on the base-board with wood screws, the side pieces forming the end of the box when the game board is closed. Hinged to these stationary side pieces are two extensions that complete the sides of the game board when it is in use. These are held rigidly to the edge of the end panel that comes directly under the tripod, by means of bolts and wing nuts—two on one extension and one on the other. Notches in the edge of the end panels permit the bolts to be slipped in place readily. Besides serving the purpose of attaching the extensions rigidly, the bolts also hold the feet of the tripod. When the game board is to be folded, the bolts are loosened,

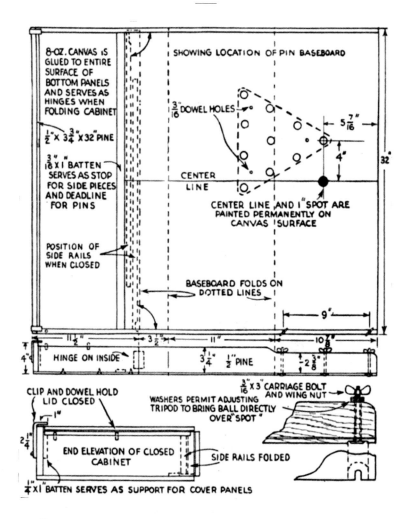

8-OZ. CANVAS IS GLUED TO ENTIRE SURFACE OF BOTTOM PANELS AND SERVES AS HINGES WHEN FOLDING CABINET

$\frac{1}{2}$" X 3$\frac{3}{4}$" X 32" PINE

$\frac{3}{16}$" X 1" BATTEN SERVES AS STOP FOR SIDE PIECES AND DEADLINE FOR PINS

POSITION OF SIDE RAILS WHEN CLOSED

SHOWING LOCATION OF PIN BASEBOARD

$\frac{3}{16}$" DOWEL HOLES

CENTER LINE

CENTER LINE AND 1" SPOT ARE PAINTED PERMANENTLY ON CANVAS SURFACE

5$\frac{7}{16}$"

4"

32"

BASEBOARD FOLDS ON DOTTED LINES

9"

11$\frac{1}{2}$"   3$\frac{1}{2}$"   11"   10$\frac{1}{8}$"

HINGE ON INSIDE

3$\frac{1}{4}$" $\frac{1}{2}$" PINE   2$\frac{3}{8}$"

4"

CLIP AND DOWEL HOLD LID CLOSED

1"

2$\frac{1}{4}$"

END ELEVATION OF CLOSED CABINET

SIDE RAILS FOLDED

$\frac{1}{4}$" X 1" BATTEN SERVES AS SUPPORT FOR COVER PANELS

$\frac{3}{16}$" X 3" CARRIAGE BOLT AND WING NUT

WASHERS PERMIT ADJUSTING TRIPOD TO BRING BALL DIRECTLY OVER "SPOT"

DETAILS OF ASSEMBLY AND ARRANGEMENT SHOWING THE SIMPLICITY OF CONSTRUCTION. IN PLAYING, THE PINS KNOCKED DOWN BY EACH SWING ARE GATHERED INTO THE SPACE BEHIND THE SLAT THAT SERVES AS A DEADLINE.

the tripod is removed, and the extensions are folded together. This way they will be next to each other, against a cross batten that is screwed down permanently and bears the following instruction: "Gather All Toppled Pins Back on This Slat Before Making Second Swing." Other details on the construction and assembly of the game board, such as the clip-and-dowel arrangement for holding the box closed, can be

obtained by going over the drawings. The centerline and the ball suspension spot are marked with black ink or paint. Now for the accessories to the

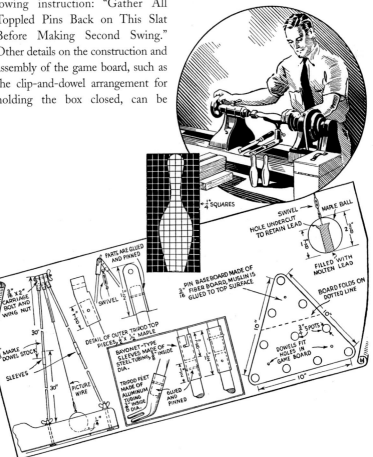

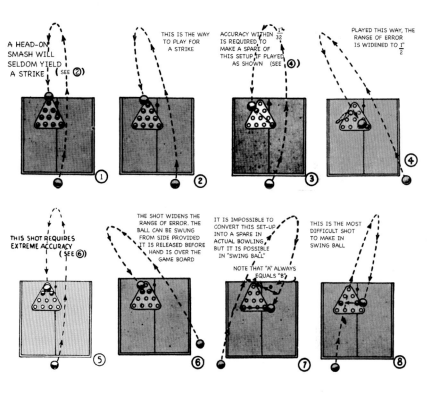

game: The belly of the pins is 1 7/16 in. in diameter, so they can be turned readily from 1½ x 1½-in. stock. Maple is particularly recommended, but beech, mahogany, or Australian gum can also be used. The ball is turned from maple or lignum-vitae, although a billiard ball also serves the purpose. When a maple ball is used, it is heavily weighted with

metal, as shown in one of the details. The hole is enlarged at its base to retain the metal, which is poured when it is barely above its melting point, in order to avoid scorching the wood. The construction of the tripod is clearly illustrated. Bayonet-type sleeves are necessary on the legs, because the oscillations of the ball put a strain on the legs that would work straight ferrules loose. A swivel at the top of the tripod holds a length of picture wire from which the ball is suspended, another swivel being provided at the ball end. The pin baseboard folds as indicated by the dotted lines in one of the details. It is fitted with three dowels that are glued in place and project on the underside so that they can be set into holes drilled in the surface of the game board. This assures the correct position of the pins at all times.

Now, let's play swing ball. First, the tripod legs must be adjusted to bring the ball directly over the sus-pension spot, and the wire adjusted to hold the ball ¼ in. off the game board. *Figs. 1* to *8* illustrate a few of the swings or "shots." Strangely, a strike will seldom result from a head-on hit of the kingpin. *Fig. 2* shows the more scientific way to go after a strike. Two-pin shots will crop up constantly in the play, and the player most adept at making them, thereby recording a spare, is the girl who will win the most games, other factors begin equal. Careful playing, with application to the technique of making the spares count, will aid materially in shooting a higher score.

— A MARBLE-UNDER-BRIDGE GAME OF SKILL —

The object of this game is to pass a marble from one end to the other of the "roadway," under the "bridges," and over the "inclines," without dropping it. A stop must be made at each hole. The device is made as follows: Cut two pieces of wood, ¼ by 1¾ by 12 in., and join them to form a right angle. Cut 4 pieces of cardboard, 1¾ by 2½ in. wide, with a ¾-in. hole in the center, for inclines *I*, and 4 pieces that are 1¾ by 3 in., for bridges, *A;* also two pieces 1¾ in. square for stops, *C*.

Fasten them with tacks as shown. The marble should be large enough so that it will rest in the holes at *B*.

— THE MAGNETIC THEATER —

An evening's entertainment can be crafted and executed in the same evening with the family working together on a magnetic theater. Cutout figures on paper clips or small pieces of iron are moved across the stage with a magnet held under the stage floor. The stage is lighted with a small flashlight battery and bulb. The whole theater is constructed, as shown, and is easily put together in under an hour. Performances are the product of the producers' imaginations.

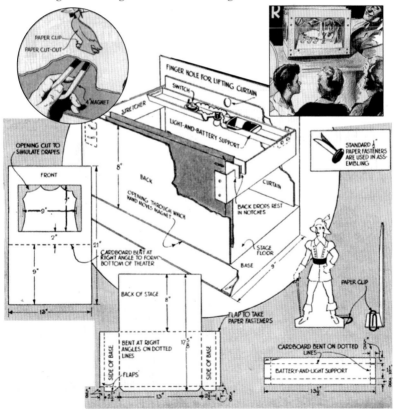

— REGULATION SIZE TENNIS TABLE —

This well-built tennis table of regulation size has a ⅜-in. plywood top made from two 3-by-8-ft. sheets. It is fastened with ¾-in. screws at 6-in. intervals. All screw holes are countersunk, filled with plastic wood, and sanded smooth. After finishing the top, it is painted a dull dark green with a ¾-in. white stripe around the edge and along the center lengthwise.

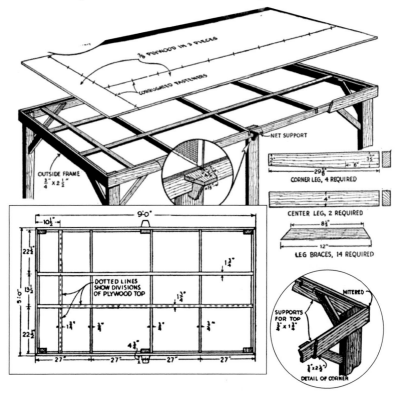

OUTSIDE FRAME ¾" x 2½"

NET SUPPORT

CORNER LEG, 4 REQUIRED

CENTER LEG, 2 REQUIRED

LEG BRACES, 14 REQUIRED

DOTTED LINES SHOW DIVISIONS OF PLYWOOD TOP

SUPPORTS FOR TOP ¾" x 1¾"

MITERED

DETAIL OF CORNER

⅜ PLYWOOD IN 3 PIECES

CORRUGATED FASTENERS

— A 3-D Tic-Tac-Toe Game —

Crafters who like relatively simple projects that can be completed in an evening, or over a weekend at the most, will find this project ideal. It can be easily made from readily available materials. And the simplicity means that the daughter of the family can help out even before play begins.

This four-in-one version of a

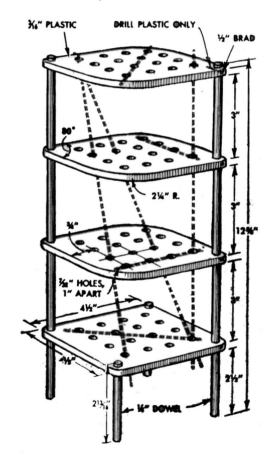

children's popular game is a good example of a project that can also be an excellent gift. The object of the game is to align four pegs in a row, using any combination similar to the ones indicated by the dotted lines in the illustration. Each player has 32 pegs of a color different from those of her opponent. Wooden or

plastic golf tees will do for the pegs. The four tiers of the board can be made of clear or colored transparent plastic. The tiers may be cut square or diamond shape, making the acute angles 80 degrees. The diamond shape facilitates inserting the pegs in

the center holes of the lower tiers. Perfect alignment of the 16 holes in each tier with those in the other tiers can be assured by drilling the four pieces simultaneously. The dowel uprights are pinned to the tiers with small brads at the corners.

{ CHAPTER 5 }

THE SPORTING GIRL

—

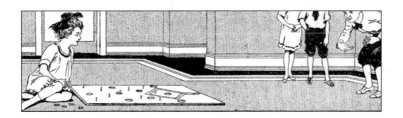

MAKE *a* SPLASH!

— SWIMMING UNDER WATER —

The following instructions, when carefully followed, will enable any girl who can swim to practically double the length of time she can remain underwater. The usual method of nearly all swimmers is to take the deepest breath possible before plunging. They generally swim in a haphazard way, and come to the top just as soon as they think they are running out of breath.

To break one's own record, one should observe the following rules: First, take several deep breaths, and then blow every particle of air out of the lungs. Instantly draw in a full, deep breath, and then dive, going down deeper than usual. Second, take regular strokes, about one per second, and always try to go one stroke farther than in the last dive. By counting the number of strokes taken under the water, the swimmer's confidence is wonderfully increased. She is also able to accurately judge her location at all times.

The ability of a person to remain under water can be tested on land by practicing the above method and timing herself with a watch. This is the method used by most professional swimmers.

— MAKING A DIVING SPRINGBOARD —

Make a springboard for the swimming pool or the "old swimming hole" that actually has "spring" to it. This is made by connecting three boards somewhat after the manner in which the leaves of an automobile spring are assembled. In this way the spring obtained is much greater than that produced by any single board.

The top board is the longest, the next is about 3 ft. shorter, and the lowest one is about 4 ft. shorter than the second. The inner ends of the

A HIGHLY SATISFACTORY DIVING SPRINGBOARD MADE BY BOLTING THREE PLANKS TOGETHER

boards are set flush. All three are fastened together throughout with screws, and at the points illustrated with iron clamps. The clamps should be as unyielding as possible and made with sufficient space between the ends so that the boards can be clamped together tightly. The clamps are fitted into grooves cut on the underside of the bottom and middle boards, but the upper surface is not countersunk.

— Non-Slip Diving Board —

The slippery surface of a wet diving board is often the cause of injury to swimmers, so you can employ this very simple and practical method for making the boards at the pool slip-proof. A number of rubber bands, about 2 in. wide, were cut from discarded inner tubes and snapped over the board, spaced about 1 in. apart. This provides enough friction to prevent the divers from slipping.

— Build Yourself a "Water Sprite" —

A sport that has experienced a great wave of popularity at lake and ocean resorts is that of aquaplaning—riding on a board towed by a motorboat. One ride is sufficient to convert any citizen into an enthusiastic fan.

AQUAPLANES IN ACTION.

Anyone with a basic set of tools can with ease and pleasure make a "water sprite," as the aquaplanes have been nicknamed. A girl working with a grown-up's aid and exercising reasonable care will be able to create one that is quite as good as a commercial board.

Experimentation has shown that

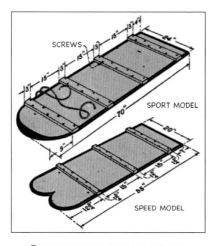

SCREWS

SPORT MODEL

SPEED MODEL

CONSTRUCTION DETAILS OF THE "WATER SPRITES" OR AQUAPLANES.

though the real thrill comes at higher speeds. The speed model—and the sport type when it is carrying two passengers—requires about double this speed.

Dimensions for both types are given in the drawing. There is nothing arbitrary about these sizes, and they may be varied at will. But as they have been found satisfactory, there would be no point in departing too far from these specifications, unless the material available made it necessary. If the sprite is too narrow, it will be very nearly impossible to stay on. On the other hand, it should not be too wide. Any smooth, unsplintered wood may be used for the board part on which the rider stands, or tries to stand. The boards shown were made of tongue-and-groove white-pine stock, clamped up with marine glue in the joints and strengthened by cleats. Such elaborate joints are an entirely unnecessary refinement, and were used only to improve the looks of the finished sprite.

It will be quite satisfactory to hold the boards together by three or four cleats running across. These should be held firmly in place by flat-head countersunk wood screws, staggered

two sizes offer the most satisfaction, the sport model and the speed model. The former is a larger plane, capable of being towed by a slower boat and carrying as many as three passengers. The latter is a smaller board that, having less area exposed to the water, must be drawn faster in order to plane with its single passenger. It offers the greatest kick of the two styles, because it travels faster and requires greater skill in balancing and riding. The larger or sport model—family model one spectator called it—will plane with one passenger at a speed of 6 miles an hour,

to distribute the strain. Because the water sprite receives a great deal of pounding while in use, all precautions should be taken to make it as strong as possible. The edges of the cleats should be beveled, because the rider braces her feet against them. Similarly, the edges of the board should be beveled, as the rider will find herself grasping at the side to climb back on, after inevitably losing her balance. The towrope should be passed through holes bored into the forward cleat and under this part, for greater strength, in the speed model, and the second cleat in the sport model. The rope to which the rider holds should be put through holes in front of the towline. Each rope is held by a knot on the end. The towline is led out on the bottom side of the board, and knotted on top. The sprite may be finished with clear varnish or painted in color. The natural wood finish presents a more professional-looking job, while the board in use, has the appearance of snap and life if painted in brilliant colors. You can further embellish the design with seagulls, a mermaid or other decoration such as a racing stripe.

In use, the water sprite runs 15 to 20 ft. astern of the towing boat. Very

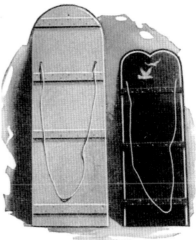

LEFT, THE SPORT MODEL FOR ONE OR MORE PERSONS; RIGHT: THE SPEED MODEL FOR ONE RIDER.

little in the way of instructions can be offered for riding the board, because it is largely a matter of experience. A good practice is to lie flat on the board, taking a short hold on the hand rope and allowing plenty of slack cord, between the stomach and the sprite. As it gains speed, slide back, keeping the weight well aft. If the weight is too far forward, the stern will tip up, the bow will dive and the entire board will spin around. As the sprite assumes full speed, assume a squatting, then a standing position. Practice will enable the rider to do various stunts.

PERFECT-10 GYMNASTICS

— AN OUTDOOR GYMNASIUM:
THE HORIZONTAL BAR —

Gymnastic apparatus costs money and needs to be housed, because it will not stand the weather. Gymnasiums are not always available for the average girl who likes exercise and who would like to learn the tricks on horizontal and parallel bars, horse, and rings, which all young athletes are taught in regular gymnastic courses.

Any small crowd of girls—even two—having a few simple tools, a will to use them, and the small amount of money required to buy the necessary wood, bolts, and rope, can make a first-class gymnasium. If trees are convenient, and someone can swing an axe, the money outlay will be almost nothing. The following plans are for material purchased from a mill squared and cut to length. To substitute small, straight trees for the squared timbers requires but little change to the plans.

The most important piece of apparatus in the gymnasium is the horizontal bar. Most gymnasiums have two: one adjustable bar for various exercises, and a high bar strictly for gymnastic work. The outdoor gymnasium combines the two. The material required is as follows: 2 pieces of wood, 4 in. square by 9½ ft.-long; 4 pieces, 2 by 4 in. by 2 ft. long; 4 pieces, 1 by 7 in. by 6½ ft. long; 4 filler pieces, ¾ by 3 in. by 3 ft. 9 in. long; and 1 piece, 2½ in. square by 5 ft. 7 in. long. This latter piece is for the bar and should be of well-seasoned, straight-grained hickory. It makes no difference what kind of wood is used for the other pieces, but it is best to use cedar for the heavy pieces that are set in the ground, because it will take years for this wood to rot. Ordinary yellow pine will also do very well. The four 7-in. boards should be of some hardwood if possible, such as oak, hickory, maple, chestnut or ash. The other material necessary consists of 2 bolts, ½ in. in diameter and 7 in. long; 16 screws, 3 in. long; 4 heavy screw eyes with two ½-in. shanks; 50 ft. of heavy galvanized wire; 80 ft. of ¼-in. manila rope and 4 pulley blocks. Four cleats are also required but these can be made of wood at home.

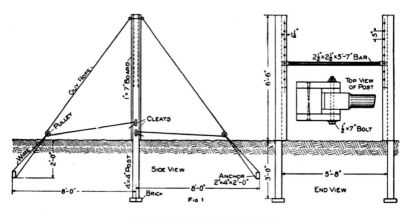

ADJUSTABLE HORIZONTAL BAR

Draw a line on the four 7-in. boards along the side of each from end to end, 1¼ in. from one edge. Beginning at one end of each board make pencil dots on this line 5 in. apart for a distance of 3 ft. 4 in. Bore holes through the boards on these marks with a 9/16-in. bit. Fasten two of these boards on each post with the 3-in. screws, as shown in the top view of the post in *Fig. 1*, forming a channel of the edges in which the holes were bored. Two of the filler pieces are fastened in each channel as shown, so as to make the space fit the squared end of the bar snugly. The ends of the boards with the holes should be flush with the top of the post. This will make each pair of

holes in the 7-in. boards coincide, so the ½-in. bolt can be put through them and the squared end of the bar.

Select a level place where the apparatus is to be placed and dig two holes 6 ft. apart, each 3 ft. deep, and remove all loose dirt. The ends of the posts not covered with the boards are set in these holes on bricks or small stones. The channels formed by the boards must be set facing each other with the inner surfaces of the posts parallel and 5 ft. 8 in. apart. The holes around the posts are filled with earth and well tamped.

The hickory piece that is to form the bar should be planed, scraped and sandpapered until it is perfectly smooth and round except for 3 in. at

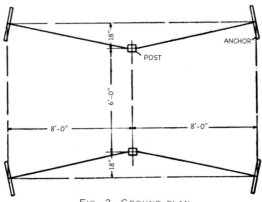

FIG. 2. GROUND PLAN

each end. Bore a ⁹/₁₆-in. hole through each square end 1¼ in. from the end. The bar may be fastened at any desired height by slipping the ½-in. bolts through the holes bored in both the bar and channel.

Each post must be well braced to keep it rigid while a person is swinging on the bar. Four anchors are placed in the ground at the corners of an imaginary rectangle 9 by 16 ft., in the center of which the posts stand, as shown in *Fig. 2.* Each anchor is made of one 2-ft. piece of wood, around the center of which four strands of the heavy galvanized wire are twisted, then buried to a depth of 2 ft., the extending ends of the wires coming up to the surface at an angle.

The heavy screw eyes are turned into the posts at the top and lengths of ropes tied to each. These ropes, or guys, pass through the pulley blocks, which are fastened to the projecting ends of the anchor wire, and return to the posts where they are tied to cleats. Do not tighten the guy ropes without the bar in place, because to do so will strain the posts in the ground. Do not change the elevation of the bar without slacking up on the ropes. It takes but little pull on the guy ropes to make them taut, and once tightened the bar will be rigid.

Oil the bar when it is finished and remove it during the winter. It is wise to oil the wood occasionally during the summer and reverse the bar regularly to prevent its becoming curved. The wood parts should be well painted to protect them from the weather.

— AN OUTDOOR GYMNASIUM: PARALLEL BARS —

Parallel bars hold a high place in the affection of those girls who frequent gymnasiums as the best apparatus for development of the back and shoulder muscles, as well as a promoter of ease and grace of movement. The outdoor gym can have a set of these bars with very little more labor than was required for the horizontal bar.

The materials required are as follows: 4 posts, preferably cedar, 4 in. square and 6 ft. long; 2 base pieces, 4 in. square and 5½ ft. long; 2 cross braces, 2 by 4 in. by 7 ft. 8 in. long; 4 knee braces, 2 by 4 in. by 3 ft. 8 in. long; 2 bars of straight grained hickory, 2 by 3 in. by 10 ft. long; 4 wood screws, 6 in. long; 4 bolts, 8 in. long; 8 bolts 7 in. long; and 1 dozen large spikes.

To make the apparatus, lay off the bases, as shown in the end view, and bevel the ends at an angle of 60 degrees. Chisel out two notches 4 in. wide and 1 in. deep, beginning at a point 9 in. from either side of the center. These are to receive the lower ends of the posts. Bevel two sides of one end of each post down to the width of the finished bar—a little less than 2 in. Cut notches in these ends to receive the oval bars. Bevel the ends of the knee braces, as shown in the diagram, and fasten the lower ends to the beveled ends of the bases with the spikes. Fasten the upper ends of the knee braces to the uprights with the 8-in. bolts put through the holes bored for that purpose, and countersink the heads. Lay the whole end flat on the ground and make a mark 2½ ft. from the bottom of the base up along the posts. Fasten the end braces with their top edges flush with the marks, using four of the 7-in. bolts. Finally toe-nail the base into the ends of the posts merely to hold them in position while the whole structure is being handled.

Two end pieces must be made. These sets or ends of the apparatus are to be buried in trenches dug to the depth of 2½ ft., with a distance between the two inner surfaces of the posts, which face each other, of 7 ft. After the trenches are dug, additional long, shallow trenches must be made connecting the posts to receive the side braces. The function of these side braces is to hold both ends together solidly. It is necessary to

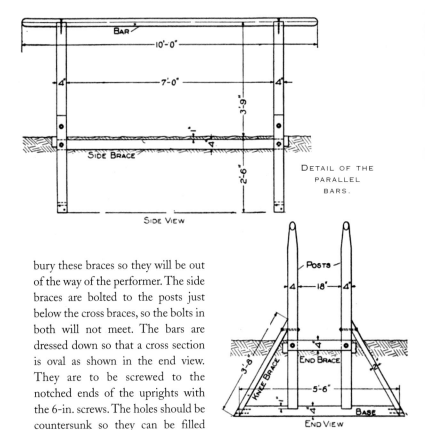

Detail of the parallel bars.

Side View

End View

bury these braces so they will be out of the way of the performer. The side braces are bolted to the posts just below the cross braces, so the bolts in both will not meet. The bars are dressed down so that a cross section is oval as shown in the end view. They are to be screwed to the notched ends of the uprights with the 6-in. screws. The holes should be countersunk so they can be filled with putty after the screws are in place. The bars should be well oiled with linseed oil to protect them from the weather, and in the winter they would be removed and stored.

Every piece of wood in this apparatus can be round and cut from trees, except the bars. If using mill-cut lumber, leave it undressed. And if using round timber, leave the bark on it as a protection from the weather. It is wise to paint the entire apparatus, save the bars, before burying the lower part of the end pieces. The wood, so treated, will last for years, but even unpainted they are very durable. Be sure to tamp down the earth well about the posts. A smooth piece of ground should be selected on which to erect the apparatus.

— AN OUTDOOR GYMNASIUM: THE HORSE —

The German horse is that peculiar piece of apparatus that is partly a horizontal obstruction to leap over, partly a barrier for jumps, partly a smooth surface of long and narrow dimensions over and about which the body may slide and swing, and partly an artificial back for the purpose of a peculiar style of leap frog.

To make a horse for an outdoor gym, no difficult work is required, save the preparation of the top or body of the horse. The making of the regular gymnasium horse requires a very elaborate woodworking and leather upholstery plant, but the one used for outdoor work can be made of a log of wood. Procure from a saw mill, lumberyard, or from the woods, one half of a tree trunk from a tree 9 to 15 in. in diameter—the larger the better. The length may be anywhere from 4 to 7 ft., but 5½ ft. is a good length.

The round part of this log must be planed, scraped and sanded until it is perfectly smooth, and free from knots, projections and splinters. Hand holds must be provided next. These are placed 18 in. apart in a center position on the horse. Make two parallel saw cuts 2 in. apart, straight down in the round surface of the horse until each cut is 9 in. long. Chisel out the wood between the cuts, and in the mortises created insert the handholds. Each handhold is made of a 9-in. piece of 2 x 4 in. stud cut rounded on one edge. These are well nailed in place. The body of the horse is to be fastened on top of posts so that it may be adjusted for height. It is not as difficult to make as the horizontal and parallel bars.

The materials required are as follows: Two posts, 4 in. square by 5 ft. long; 2 adjusting pieces, 2 by 4 in. by 3 ft. 3 in. long; 1 cross brace, 2 by 4 in. by 3 ft. long; 2 bases, 4 in. square by 5½ ft. long; 4 knee braces, 2 by 4 in. by 3 ft. long; two ½-in. bolts, 9 in. long, to fasten the knee braces at the top; ten ½-in. bolts,

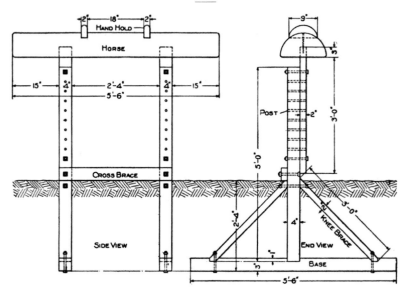

THE GERMAN HORSE.

7 in. long, 4 to fasten the knee braces at the bottom, 2 to fasten the cross brace, and 4 to be used in fastening the adjusting pieces to the posts.

To construct, lay out the bases as shown in the drawing, making the mortises to receive the bottom ends of the posts exactly in the center, and cut a slanting mortise 6 in. from each end to receive the ends of the knee braces. Bevel the ends of the knee braces and fasten the upper ends of each pair to the post with one 9-in. bolt. Fasten the lower ends to the base with the 7-in. bolts.

The upper end of each post should have ⅝-in. holes bored through it parallel to the base at intervals of 3 in., beginning 1? in. from the top and extending down its length for 2 ft. 4½ in. The adjusting pieces are to be bored in a similar manner after which they are to be mortised into the underside of the horse top 15 in. from each end, and secured with screws put through the top and into the end of the adjusting pieces.

The bases with their posts and knee braces are buried 2 ft. 4 in. in the ground, parallel to each other and the same distance apart as the adjusting pieces are mortised in the horse top. When the ground has been filled in and tamped hard, the cross brace should be bolted in position with its lower edge resting on the ground and connecting the two posts.

The height of the horse from the ground is adjusted by changing the bolts in the different holes connecting the two adjusting pieces with the two posts.

Many pleasant and healthful gymnastic exercises can be had in competitive horse jumping and leaping. The handles provide a way to make many different leaps through, over, and around, including not only those made to see who can go over the horse from a standing or running start at the greatest height, but who can go over at the greatest height when starting from the "toeing off mark" farthest away from the horse. This horse should be located on level ground having smooth space about it for several feet. Of course, it goes without saying that the horse should be surrounded by a very soft, forgiving surface, such as several inches of firm foam padding, or a pit of equally soft material for landing.

THE GIRL ARCHER

— A VERSATILE HOMEMADE BOW SIGHT —

This simple, lightweight device has all the adjustable variations of an expensive bow sight. With an average-weight bow, it is fairly accurate for distances well over 100 yards. Cut from a strip of cork gasket material 1 in. wide by 6 in. long, the sight is fastened with adhesive tape to the back of the bow just above the leather grip. After gluing the cork in place, put a strip of tape on the belly of the bow opposite the cork. Stick a 2-in.

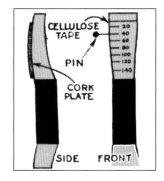

round-head pin into the cork so that the head projects ½ in. beyond the left edge of the bow. Then, by the trial-and-error method at various distances, determine the proper position of the pin for each distance and mark these positions in ink on the tape, numbering them accordingly. A coat of clear shellac will protect both the cork and the scale.

— SIGHT ON ARCHERY BOW IMPROVES YOUR AIM —

Taped to your archery bow, this adjustable sight will prove to be a more satisfactory method of shooting an arrow than the "point-of-aim" method, because you aim right at the bull's-eye instead of sighting at a marker on the ground in front of the target. Thus, any variation in bowing or in distance is not likely to affect your aim. The parts of the sight are made of heavy sheet-steel or brass, and are cut to the shape and sizes given in the detail. When finished, they should be polished with fine emery cloth or steel wool. Nickel or chromium plating will improve their appearance. The sight is mounted on the back of the bow with the sight end of the cross bar extending to the left. It is adjustable

either vertically or horizontally. Once set for a certain shooting distance, the sight may be marked so that when the same distance is shot again, the correct adjustment can be made without any trouble.

— BAMBOO BOW AND ARROW —

Almost every girl, at some time or other, would like to try her skill with a bow and arrow, but it can be rather difficult to obtain a satisfactory piece of wood for the bow. Seasoned hickory is usually recommended, but an excellent substitute is bamboo from a cheap fishing pole. With reasonable care and the help of a caring parent, a 5-ft. length of bamboo may be split into pieces of smaller dimensions, twelve or fifteen being obtained from a pole 1½ in. in diameter. After splitting it, the pieces of heart or

STRONG, DURABLE BOWS AND ARROWS CAN
BE MADE FROM BAMBOO FISHING POLES

hardened pith at the joints should be removed with a knife or plane so that the strips can be bound together in a compact bundle. The binding is a very particular part of the work, if the bow is to be made serviceable for any considerable length of time. Waxed cord should be used for this purpose. To begin, bind the middle section on the bundle to a distance of 6 in. on either side of the exact center. After fastening the string ends, cut away one-fourth of the number of sticks in the bundle just beyond the wrapping. Bind those remaining at points about 16 in. from the center of the bow. Cut away as many sticks as before and bind again, proceeding in this way until ¼ of the sticks of the bundle remain. These are bound at the tip ends, and the bow is ready to receive the string. If the work has been done carefully, the result will be a well-balanced bow that will last for years, especially if the bowstring is loosened after using it, so that the bamboo may straighten again and retain its elasticity. Serviceable arrows may also be made of similar material by binding four of the narrow strips together and inserting balancing feathers.

— MAKING ARROWS VISIBLE —

To locate your archery arrows easily after shooting them, wrap bands of tinfoil on the shafts just in front of the feathers, and shellac the bands to prevent tearing. The tinfoil will glisten in the sun so that an arrow can be seen at a distance of many yards. This method is especially effective in cases where the arrows happen to fall in tall grass weeds, etc.

{ C H A P T E R   6 }

WONDER-FULL
TOYS

MAGIC MUSIC MAKERS

— TOY MERRY-GO-ROUND WITH MUSIC —

The toy merry-go-round shown in the drawing on the next page has most of the characteristics of the real thing: it "runs," has animals, and music. The music and operating power are furnished by a child's phonograph.

The handle of a child's umbrella is cut to a convenient length, and the ends of the ribs are bent up, as shown. A simple wooden support is made, large enough to hold a good-size spool. Holes are drilled in the top and bottom of this support, to accommodate the handle of the umbrella, which extends about ½ in. below the spool pulley. The bottom end of the handle is slightly pointed, to make an easier bearing in the bottom hole of the support.

The upper part of the merry-go-round is made from the bottom of an old hat box. Oblong holes are cut in the sides, to allow two flaps to bend inward. These flaps are fastened to the umbrella ribs, by vertical slits cut in the ends. The hat-box lid, with a round piece cut from its center, forms the platform; this is suspended from the umbrella wires by slender sticks, each having a bent pin at the upper end, to hook over the wires. A pin is driven through the lower end of each stick, to support the platform. Animal pictures are cut out and glued to the sticks. The merry-go-round is elevated to the same level as the phonograph turntable. A spool is fitted over the turntable spindle of the instrument, and a ½-in. tape belt is used to drive the merry-go-round, as shown in the illustration.

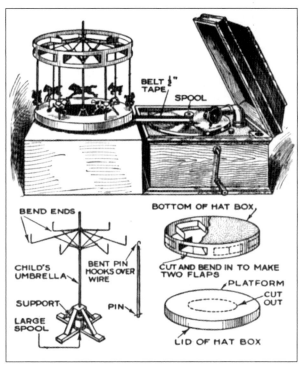

NO AMUSEMENT DEVICE BRINGS MORE JOY TO CHILDREN THAN THE MERRY-GO-ROUND.

— MUSICAL MERRY-GO-ROUND —

Music and motion are cleverly combined in this toy, which should keep young children interested for a good length of time. In the merry-go-round, which is crank-operated, a small music box of the type often used in ladies' powder boxes or jewelry cases provides the sound effects every youngster likes. *Fig. 1* gives the plan view showing the location of the music box and rollers on which the circular platform rotates. The sectional view in *Fig. 2* and the cutaway in *Fig. 3* indicate the

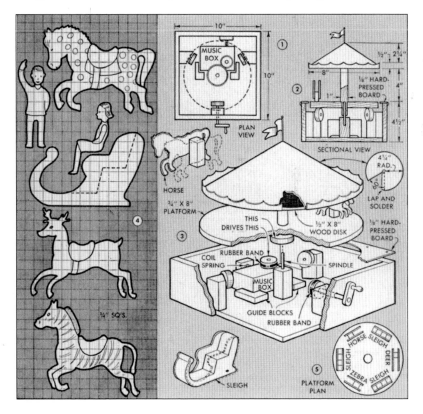

general assembly of the toy. Note that one of the rollers is fitted with a crank and is wrapped with a rubber band to provide a friction drive for the platform. A roller on the platform drives a small roller on the music box, the latter roller being wrapped with a rubber band to produce a friction drive. *Fig. 4* suggests a sleigh and animal cutouts, and *Fig. 5* shows their relative positions on the platform. Mount the animals in pairs with each sleigh just as they appear on real merry-go-rounds.

ENTERTAINING TOY TIME

— WOODEN MAN ON A STRING —

When you know the secret command, this little man will slide down the string or stop when you tell him to. But for anyone else he'll only slide and refuse to stop until he reaches the bottom of the string. The real secret lies in the position of the dowel that fastens the two arms. There is a hole drilled in it through which the string passes, and if this hole is aligned as shown in detail *A*, it will be impossible to stop the toy. However, if the hole is out of alignment, as shown in detail *B*, the man will slide when there is little tension on the string and stop when it is pulled tight. Care must be taken to be sure that the dowel is a tight fit in the body for

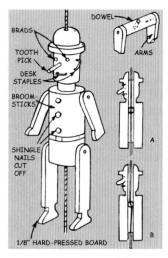

the toy to work properly. The man is carved from a broomstick and he has hard-pressed-board arms and legs. Shingle nails, staples, brads and a toothpick serve as features and decoration. Gaily colored enamels will give the toy an attractive appearance.

— SCOOTER STEERING POST PIVOTS ON A DOOR HINGE —

This skate-wheel scooter has a pivoted steering post unlike the usual homemade type. A block of 2-in. stock supports the steering post, both block and post being slotted to take a heavy butt-type hinge, which is held in place with stove bolts. The lower end of the steering post and the rear-axle block, both of hardwood, are the same width as the axle supports on the skates. This makes it an easy matter to slip the skate-wheel axles through the holes and attach the wheels. A filler block is used to close the lower end of the slot in the steering post. For the handle, a 10-in. length of broomstick is inserted in a hole drilled in the steering post and a wood screw is driven in to secure it.

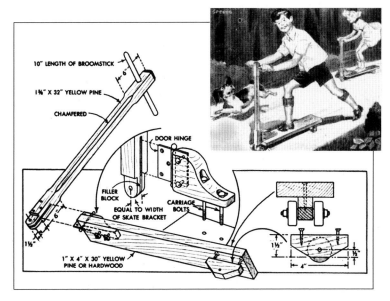

A DOOR HINGE PROVIDES A SIMPLIFIED STEERING PIVOT EASY TO INSTALL ON ANY TYPE OF HOMEMADE SCOOTER, WHETHER YOU USE ROLLER-SKATES OR OTHER WHEELS.

— BALLOON-POWERED ACTION TOYS ARE AMUSING —

Action and plenty of it is what you get with these toys which run on air supplied by small rubber balloons. The racing horse on the next page is just one of the many variations. A small air turbine is the heart of each toy, and can be assembled quickly from cardboard, a cork disk from a bottle top and a piece of soft wood. The base of the turbine is fitted with a mouthpiece at one end and a tube for attaching the balloon at the other. The mouthpiece has a paper disk attached at one end with a drop of glue to serve as a check valve to direct the escaping air from the balloon through the air vent. Care must be taken to locate the vent so that the air strikes the turbine at the cor-

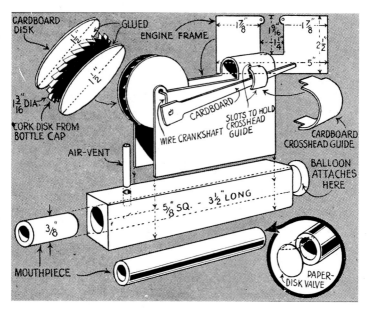

COMPONENTS OF THE MINIATURE AIR TURBINE

rect angle. A turbine is made for each toy or, if desired, figures and backgrounds can be detachable so that one turbine can be used for different toys. The figure of the racing horse is pivoted to the end of the crankshaft, which gives it a revolving motion. For some toys, slots can be made in the backgrounds and the figures attached to the connecting rod of the turbine to give them a reciprocating motion. The toys can be made to operate slowly or rapidly by pinching the neck of the balloon to regulate the air supply.

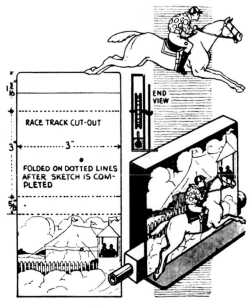

THE DYNAMIC DIORAMA

— "MOVING-PICTURE" TOY FOR CHILDREN —

A very interesting "moving-picture" toy for the small child can be made of cigar boxes, some wire, babbitt, and a few pieces of pipe can.

A rectangular opening is cut in the bottom of the cigar box (one made to contain 100 cigars). A piece of window glass or plastic is cut to fit, placed behind the opening and held in place by tacks. A frame made of cigar-box wood, shown in the illustrations, fits neatly into the box. This holds the picture ribbon against the glass and carries the spools on which the ribbon is wound. A piece of pipe cane is mounted at each corner of the frame to serve as a roller.

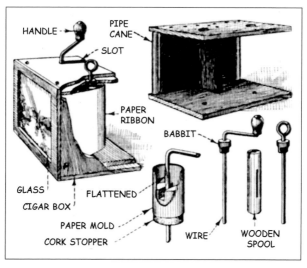

A "MOVING-PICTURE" TOY FOR THE SMALL CHILD, THAT IS
INSTRUCTIVE AS WELL AS AMUSING AND THAT CAN BE
VERY EASILY MADE FROM SCRAP MATERIALS.

The spindles, one of which has a crank formed on one end, are made of No. 9 galvanized wire, and are provided with babbitt "keys" to turn the wooden spools on which the ribbon is wound. To make these keys, a portion of the wire should be flattened, as shown. A groove is cut in the top and a hole drilled through the center of a cork stopper. Then it is pushed onto the wire directly underneath the flattened portion. A cup is formed by wrapping heavy paper around this cork, into which the babbitt can be poured. The wooden spools upon which the ribbon is wound can be made from old film spools, cut at one end to fit the babbitt key.

Children can be amused for hours with this little toy, which can be made to be instructive as well as amusing. Pictures cut from the comic or other sections of newspapers, and pasted to the ribbon in order, make very interesting moving pictures of this kind. Of course any suitable pictures may be used.

— Make This Amusing Crazy Clown —

Exceptionally odd in appearance and action, this clown will prove popular with children and will also provide amusement for their elders. If placed on an inclined board, the toy will creep down of its own accord in a peculiar way. It is operated by gravity and has

PIVOT POINT

no springs, rubber bands, or other mechanical means to give it motion.

Care should be taken to cut it out accurately and balance it correctly. To make this task an easy one we are providing full-size templates of the body and arms. The body is cut out of a piece of ¾-in. wood. Lay the template and a sheet of carbon

Drill two smaller holes in the "elbows" to receive a short length of wire. This connects the arms so that they move together and also limits their swing. The holes should not be drilled entirely through the arms but only deep enough to hold the wire snugly.

After boring a small hole at the pivot point, screw the arms to the body and slip a washer over the end of the screw before driving it in, to reduce friction between the arms and the body. Allow the arms to swing freely. The toy is then ready to be tested.

paper on the wood and trace the outline, taking care to locate the pivot point exactly. Then trace the two arms on ½-in. wood in the same way. Any close-grained wood, such as poplar, which can easily be cut and does not crack readily, may be used. The cutting is done with a jigsaw. If this is not available, use an ordinary coping saw. After the sawing has been done, sand the edges and sides and drill a hole through the pivot point on the arms to take a 1-in. round-head wood screw loosely.

Hold the figure down so that the chin and the point A touch the inclined board. In this position, the arms should swing freely and just clear the board underneath. In some cases there may be too much space between the legs and the board so that it is necessary to reduce the bulge at *A* by sanding slightly. However, if the body and legs are exactly made according to the template there will be no trouble. After the test the toy is taken apart and painted, care being observed not to get paint in the holes in the arms. If this happens the holes should be thoroughly cleaned out before reassembling. Lacquer is recommended for painting, because it dries quickly. The toy may not operate well on the first trial due to irregularities in the cutting, but a little experimental work with sandpaper on the bulge *A*, or the bottom surfaces of the arms, will usually remedy this.

— SAVINGS BANK
FILLED BY EFFICIENT "CASHIER" —

A great way for a parent to spend time with his daughter and teach her the value of money is to craft an amusing interactive bank such as this one. Any one of these examples you choose will gladly receive your savings on a tray and deposit them regularly in the "bank." Of course, the figures are only plywood cutouts painted to represent

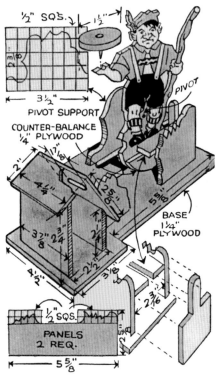

the different personalities you see pictured. Details in the illustration show how the device is assembled and how it works. When you drop a coin on the tray, the pivoted figure tilts and the coin slides off the tray and through the slot in the roof of the bank. Small

plywood weights attached to the lower end of the cutout provide a means of attaining the delicate balance necessary to keep the figure upright except when a coin is placed on the tray. The figure, the scenery, and the bank itself all should be painted in bright colors. Give the wood a coat of shellac, let it dry, then proceed with the application of the colors of your choice. When you wish to withdraw money from your "account," just remove the screws and take off the bottom of the bank.

— TWO SIMPLE AND INTERESTING TOYS —

The tiny toys described as follows offer the parent and daughter a chance to work together on toys that make wonderful gifts, or provide a fascinating diversion for the girl herself. The extension "duck pond" toy shown in the first illustration is an easily made article that, when not in use, folds compactly. The supports for the ducks, lilies, and woman are strips of soft wood, ¼ in. thick, ⅜ in. wide, and 6 in. long. Eight of these are required, and two more of the same stock, 8 in. long, for the handles. The strips are stained a gray-green color. The ducks are made of any available thin wood or veneer, sawed to shape with a coping saw,

and painted white with yellow bills. A little stud should be left extending from the base of each duck, about ¼ in. long; this is inserted into a hole drilled in the strip when assembling. The lilies are made of the same material as the ducks and colored with green stems and leaves and purple blossoms. The figure of the woman is also of the same material, and has a blue gown, brown hair and basket. The method of fastening the figure and the lilies to the strips is the same as followed for the ducks.

Lay four of the 6-in. strips and one of the 8-in. edge to edge, close together, and align them at one end. Draw a pencil line across all the

A SIMPLE "DUCK POND" TOY THAT ANY GIRL CAN MAKE.
VARIATIONS OF THE DESIGN WILL PRODUCE OTHER INTERESTING TOYS.

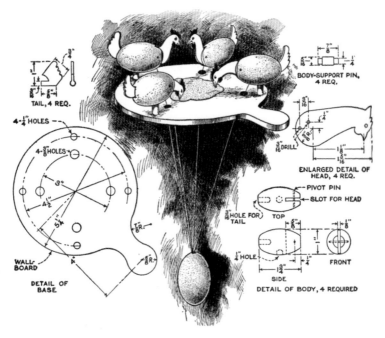

BODY-SUPPORT PIN, 4 REQ.

TAIL, 4 REQ.

4-¼" HOLES

4-⅜" HOLES

3"

4½"

5¼"

⅜" R

WALL-BOARD

DETAIL OF BASE

⅜" R

ENLARGED DETAIL OF HEAD, 4 REQ.

3/16" DRILL

PIVOT PIN

SLOT FOR HEAD

⅜" HOLE FOR TAIL

TOP

¼" HOLE

SIDE

DETAIL OF BODY, 4 REQUIRED

FRONT

"THE FEEDING CHICKENS," ANOTHER SIMPLE TOY,
THE DESIGN OF WHICH CAN ALSO BE MODIFIED TO SUIT THE MAKER.

strips, measuring ³⁄₁₆ in. from the end of the 6-in. strips. Draw a similar pencil line across the other end. Do the same with the remaining four 6-in. strips and the other 8-in. one. Draw centerlines down each of the strips. Then assemble them, as shown in the plan photo. The nails used are small brads. They are driven through the strips ⅛ in. in front of the centerline, so that the toy, when extended, will assume a circular form, instead of shooting out straight. The brads are clinched on the bottom. If small washers can be obtained and used under the heads and ends of the brads the action of the toy will be smoother. But the brads alone will serve very well if washers are unobtainable.

The interesting toy group shown in the second illustration is made to resemble four chickens, which go through the motions of feeding. The swinging of a pendulum suspended below the group causes the "head" of each of the figures to rise and descend alternately. A slight touch of the weight causes the movement to start.

The base is made of ordinary wallboard. The ¼-in. holes are made to receive the dowels that support the figures. The larger holes accommodate the strings from which the weight is suspended. The circular shape is but a suggestion. The holes, however, should be located just as shown from the center, if the sizes given for the other parts of the toy are followed.

The body of each chicken is made by turning a piece of wood to the egg-shaped form shown. Four of these are required. If a wood lathe is not available, ordinary round dowel stock of approximately the correct size may be used. Even thread spools will serve. The hole at one end is drilled 3/16 in. deep to hold the tail. The ¼-in. hole is for the supporting dowel. The slot at the end allows the head to swing freely on a pivot pin, the location of which is shown in the drawing.

Ordinary dowel stock is used for the supporting pins shown. These are glued to the bodies. The toy is assembled by pointing the heads of the chickens toward the center of the base. Glue is also used to fasten the pins firmly in the base.

The head and tail need slight explanation. Stout cardboard or light sheet metal is used for stock in making four each of these. The head pieces are pierced as shown. The lower hole is for the string that is attached to the weight. The hole slightly higher up is for the pivot pin while the top hole is the eye of the chicken. A piece of string, 9 in. long, is fastened to each of the head pieces and passed through the ⅜-in. hole in the base. Each of the head pieces is then pivoted to a body by means of a small brad driven through the body and passing through the pivot hole in the piece. The tail pieces are pressed into the holes provided for them. Paint the bodies brown, the heads white with red combs, and the tails black.

The ends of the four strings are attached to a weight below the base. Care should be taken to have the strings as nearly even in length as possible. As the pendulum swings, the heads of the chickens move up and down in a lifelike manner as long as the weight is in motion.

— How to Make a "Swimming Johnny" —

A "swimming Johnny" is an amusing toy, and one that any girl can build from odds and ends about the house. Properly assembled, it will travel several yards in calm water and can be used in the bathtub as well as outside. The body, cut from a piece of soft pine or cedar, is 8 in. long and 2 in. wide. Bevel the corners of what is to be the front end and taper the sides toward the rear as indicated. Cut out a head and taper the bottom down to a slender neck that can be fit tightly into a hole an inch from the front of the body. Cut a square hole just back of the head to take a small spool as shown. Screw a piece of brass or tin to serve as a bearing on each side of the body. Plug the spool, force a piece of stiff wire through the wood and fit the ends in the bearings, allowing them

AMUSING TOY FOR CHILDREN THAT RESEMBLES A PERSON SWIMMING

to project about ¾ in. The arms consist of two pieces of soft wood beveled on one end. The opposite ends are fitted securely over the ends of the wire axle. Be sure the bevel is uppermost when the arms are forward. Connect the spool with a long elastic band that passes below the body and attaches to a screw eye near the rear end. This should be just taut when the spool is unwound. Paint the device any suitable color and oil the spool and the wire in its bearings. The head can be painted any design desired. Wind up the elastic on the spool until it is quite tight, being sure to wind the arms to the right when the head faces left. Place "Johnny" in the water and let go of the arms. They will thrash around in an overhand stroke and push the toy ahead at good speed.

— PERPETUAL CALENDAR FOR CHILDREN DUPLICATES CYLINDER TYPE —

A perpetual calendar for a child's room, similar to the cylinder type, can be made with a few pieces of mailing tube and some scraps of wood. The tube is cut into three sections with a window in each one for the month, day and year. Three wooden dowels or other round wooden pieces, which rotate on a wire shaft, fit into the tubes and are marked for months of the year, days of the month and a series of years. The ends of the shaft are bent and fastened to a wooden base.

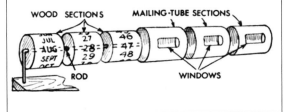

WOOD SECTIONS   MAILING-TUBE SECTIONS

JUL
AUG
SEPT
OCT

27
28
29

46
47
48

ROD   WINDOWS

ANIMAL ATTRACTION

— BIRD CAGE NOVELTY —

Assembled from strips of bamboo without using glue or nails, this novel bird cage can be made tiny enough to fit in the palm of the hand or

proportionately larger. Bowed side strips are passed through the corner frame members to hold them in place. A bamboo perch supports a balsawood bird.

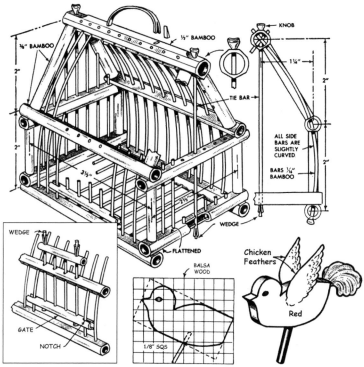

— AMUSING ANIMAL TOY
CAN CHANGE ITS FACE —

Wagged from side to side by a pendulum, the head of this toy has interchangeable eyes, mouth, nose, and ears, which can be used in various combinations to produce unusual facial expressions. Variations of these facial parts are shown in the squared detail. All parts have dowels attached for anchoring them in place, and they all fit in holes in the face except the ears, which slip into staples on the back of the head. The base for the head is a box with the front side painted to resemble the bars of a cage. As shown in the detail, the head is attached off center to a dowel, which turns in a hole through the side of the box. Washers are used as spacers between the head, box, and pendulum, which is fastened rigidly to the end of the dowel inside the box. The box of the original was painted yellow, bars black, and face with the black features.

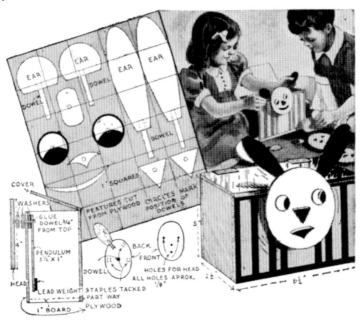

— A JOINTED PONY —

With this toy, a doting parent can give their daughter a piece of the Wild West experience. Besides being just a toy, this jointed pony and cowboy will be helpful in drawing horse silhouettes in lively, lifelike poses. The jointed parts are made to work snugly so that the pony will hold his pose when laid on paper and traced. The resulting outline, although somewhat rough, will be the approximate shape. This makes it simply a matter of blackening in the figure to create a silhouette. Working from patterns enlarged full-size from the squared profiles given, you first cut out the central section or core of the body, including the neck, head and tail. The body is built up by gluing ⅜-in. pieces to each side of the ½-in. core, applying glue to just the surfaces of the core that are fixed and seeing that the glue does not work into the joints. The ⅛-in. pieces covering the outside of the body are cut to exactly the same shape as the

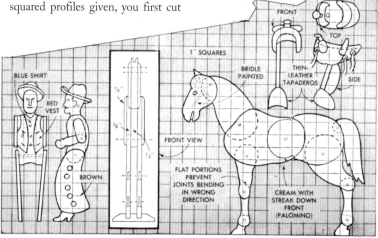

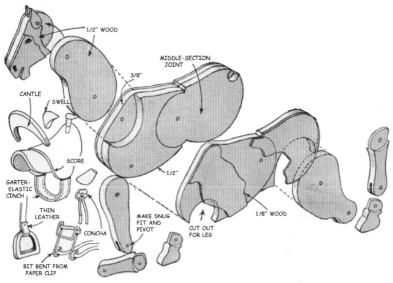

1/2" WOOD

MIDDLE-SECTION JOINT

3/8"

CANTLE

SWELL

SCORE

GARTER-ELASTIC CINCH

THIN LEATHER

CONCHA

MAKE SNUG FIT AND PIVOT

CUT OUT FOR LEG

1/2"

1/8" WOOD

BIT BENT FROM PAPER CLIP

⅜-in. pieces, except that no cutouts are made for the legs. All five sections comprising the assembly are pivoted at the center hole. The ears are a separate unit so that they can be moved. The saddle is carved as detailed, although if the pony is to be used mostly drawing, the saddle can be omitted. When attached at the angle shown, the cowboy's legs will clamp him on the pony.

— HOW YOU CAN MAKE A WIGGLING PUP —

Animated wooden toys on wheels are very popular, and are much enjoyed by children. The construction of the wiggling pup is simple and will prove an interesting pastime. The youngsters will also like so much the better because someone made it for them. The feature of the

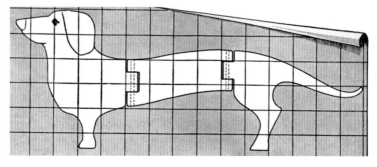

SIMPLE DESIGN FOR A TOY PUP MADE OF WOOD AND HAVING FLEXIBLE JOINTS. THE WORK OF ASSEMBLING AND PAINTING IT CAN BE DONE IN AN HOUR.

toy is its jointed body, which causes it to dart from side to side as it is pulled along on the floor.

Any close-grained wood can be used, such as poplar or white pine. A piece of 1¼-in. stock, 6 in. wide and 15 in. long, is all the wood required to make it. First, lay out the pattern on a piece of paper of that size, laid out in 1-in. squares, using the design in the accompanying illustration. Then get some carbon paper and trace the design on the wood that has been well planed. Take care that the grain of the wood runs lengthwise of the board, or the tail will be easily broken off when it receives the more or less rough handling a child is certain to give it. Then, with a coping saw, cut out the outline very

carefully. After each section is cut out, round off the corners at the joints, drill holes through them as indicated and sand the surface until it is smooth and ready for the application of paint or enamel. The axles can be made of the same stock. They are about ¾ in. square and 5 in. long. They are screwed to the feet, holes being drilled first to prevent splitting the wood. Almost any kind of wheels can be used. They are fastened to the axles with wood screws or nails, leaving them loose enough to turn easily. If one has access to a wood-turning lathe, neat wheels of the same thickness as that of the body of the pup can be turned out. A small hole is drilled through the center of the front axle for a string to

CLOTH
EAR

DETAILS OF A WIGGLING PUP,
SHOWING PIVOTED JOINTS AND FELT EARS.

pull the toy with. Get the joints to work smoothly before applying paint or enamel. By using a file on the flat surface and then rubbing a little petroleum jelly or hard oil on them, they will work very smoothly.

The natural color of the dog, which represents a dachshund, is black or brown. Glossy enamel will be found most effective on toys, and three coats of colored lacquer will give a good finish. However, if paint is handy, it can be used, and then a glossy finish can be achieved by applying a coat of varnish. Black for the axles and a bright red for the wheels will be pleasing to children. The wheels should, of course, be finished separately, and when they are put on the axle, an iron washer should be used to reduce friction between the wheel and the axle. The ears can be cut out of a piece of brown or black felt and are glued or tacked on. Nails are used for pivots on which the joints move and are cut off so that they will not project under the body. It is a good idea to counterbore the pivot holes at the top to take the nail heads.

— A Toy Horse That Walks —

Every girl dreams of her own horse and with the instructions given here, she can have it. This toy, amusing for the youngsters and their elders as well, will repay one for the making of it. Use a cigar box or balsa wood for

THE TOY IS PUSHED BY MEANS OF THE HANDLE, CAUSING THE HORSE TO WALK.

the carriage, making it about 10 in. high, and shape it in the design shown. Nail a piece of wood, ⅛ by 2 by 4 in. wide, on each side of the carriage, and drill ⅛-in. holes in them for the axle. For the horse, draw an outline of the head, neck, and body on a piece of wood, ½ by 4 by 6 in. long. Cut this out and drill ⅛-in. holes where the legs are attached.

Cut the legs as shown, about 3½ in. long. Attach them with small bolts, or rivets, allowing space to move freely. The wheels are made of pine, ½ in. thick and 3 in. in diameter. The axle is made of $3/16$-in. wire bent to the shape indicated, ½ in. at each offset. Fit the wheels on the axle tightly, so as not to turn on it, the axle turning in the pieces nailed to the sides of the carriage. The horse is attached to the top of the carriage by a strip of wood. A 3-ft. wooden handle is attached to the back of carriage to guide it. Wires are attached to the legs, connecting with the offsets in the axle.

— ❖ ❖ ❖ —

{ CHAPTER 7 }

MAKING GREAT GIFTS

—

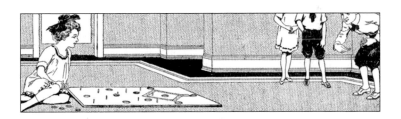

THE PERFECT PRESENT
for MOM

— FABULOUS RIBBON BOWS —

The right ribbon is the "icing on the cake" of the well-wrapped package. With a little patience and diligence, any girl can learn to wrap the type of stunning bows that seem too intricate to be made by anybody but a professional. As with many things that seem

complicated, these bows are actually fairly easy to make. They do require time and patience, and not all the first few attempts will be completely satisfactory, but you will soon find yourself proficient enough

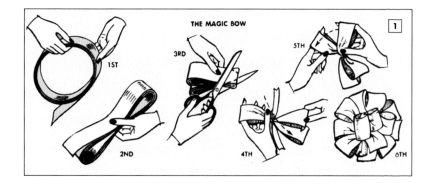

to be able to place fancy bows on all the packages you gift wrap.

Fig. 1 shows the step-by-step method of making a "magic" bow. First, a length of ribbon is formed into a fairly large loop. Second, the loop is flattened in such a manner that the loose end of the ribbon is even with the end of the flattened loop. The third step requires the flattened loop to be folded in half and a diagonal cut made across each corner at the fold. A narrow ribbon or cord then is tied around the resulting V-notches when the ribbon is unfolded, as shown in the fourth step. The ribbon is refolded, and the open loops are pulled through each other for the fifth step. The pulled-through loops are then shaped with your hands and positioned to result in the flower-like bow shown in the sixth step in *Fig. 1*.

The French bow in *Fig. 2* is formed by "piling" a number of loops, one on top of the other, then tying the loops at the center with the loose ends of the ribbon. The resulting pattern of loops is pulled out to form the bow as shown in the detail. The elongated bow, shown in *Fig. 2* is started in the same manner as the French bow, but some of the loops of the bow are cut so that there are a number of loose ends. The dahlia bow, in the lower detail of *Fig. 2* is formed in the same way as the French bow, but then all the loops are cut diagonally at their centers to provide a leaf-like appearance.

The tailored bow at the top of *Fig. 3* is formed much like the French bow, with loops being piled

one on top of the other, but each succeeding loop is made slightly shorter
than the preceding one. The free
ends of the ribbon are spread out, as
shown, and the bow tied at the center with a small ribbon, or with a
cord. The latter is available with
strands of silver, gold, and other colors woven into it, adding to the
attractiveness of the bow. The carnation bow in *Fig. 3* is started like the
magic bow in *Fig. 1*. After the loops
are pulled through each other they
are grasped in the hand and cut with
the scissors to simulate the petals of a
carnation. Fairly wide ribbon is used
for the daisy bow. The bow is started
by piling a number of loops, which
are then tied at the center. The loops
are pulled through each other, and
the finished bow is held at the center
by a thumbtack. The latter is best

when attaching the bow to a package. As shown in the detail, the two-in-one bow is simply a flattened roll of ribbon that is folded off-center and cut across the corners to form V-notches, as for the magic bow. Being off-center, the notches, when tied, cause the bow to have one end longer than the other. The loops of this bow can also be pulled apart for a different effect. Tying the informal bow starts by looping the ribbon around your thumb. Loops are then formed as shown. The bow can be left loose and fastened to a package with tape, or the ends of the ribbon can be pulled through the loop formed on the thumb, and the bow tied firmly.

After you have tied a number of the bows shown here, you might design some of your own. Using two different colors of ribbon for one bow is one method of modifying the designs shown. Bows of the same type, tied with narrow ribbon, will appear to be different when tied with wide ribbon. Using both wide and narrow ribbon, as well as two colors also makes for different appearance.

— PICTURES ARE PRETTY: 9 ATTRACTIVE FRAME DESIGNS —

Who wouldn't love any of these frames made from the heart? A grown-up will most likely have to do the more complex bending operations, but there's plenty that the reasonably handy girl can do to help craft these memorable picture holders. Simple in design, these

3/8" DOWELS ON
7/8" CENTERS

6

1/32" X 3/4" PLASTIC

plastic picture frames depend largely on the beauty and crystal clarity of the material for their effectiveness. Some of the frames, such as those in *Photos 1, 2, 3,* and *4,* use plastic for both the frame and glass. Construction details are shown in the correspondingly numbered photo and line drawings. These frames are best worked on a strip heater, which confines the bending heat to the area required. Sharp bends are worked by heating the plastic along the bending line and then rubbing the joint gently with a cloth-covered block as the

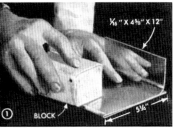

1/16" X 4 5/8" X 12"

1

BLOCK

5 1/2"

FOR A CLEAN, SHARP BEND, RUB THE HEATED PLASTIC WITH A CLOTH-COVERED BLOCK.

plastic cools. Large-radius bends are made by heating the required area and pressing the free end against any

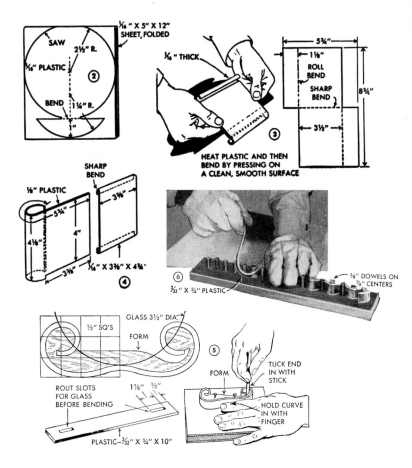

smooth, clean surface until the desired curvature is obtained. If the correct curve is not made on the first attempt, it's a simple matter to reheat the piece and repeat the bending process as often as is necessary.

Bent frames are illustrated by two simple designs, as shown *Photos 5* and *6*. This type of construction always requires a form. The form for No. 6, illustrated by *Fig. 6,* is a simple arrangement of pegs. The form for No. 5 is band-sawed to the shape shown in *Fig. 5*. The wood should be sanded until it is very smooth to prevent marks transferring to the plastic. Slots for the picture glass in design No. 5 are cut previous to bending. An overall heat, commonly obtained by placing the strip in an oven, is used for all bent frames when smooth-flowing curves are required.

Straight frames, such as shown in *Photo 7* and *Fig. 7*, are made from straight sections of plastic assembled with cemented butt joints. A solvent-type cement gives firm, clear joints on work of this kind and is easily and quickly applied. This type of frame has the edges sanded with 100-grit wet-or-dry sandpaper used with water, which gives a frosty effect that combines nicely with the crystal plastic. Alternate designs for straight frames are suggested in *Figs. 8 and 9*. The same type of assembly and construction is used.

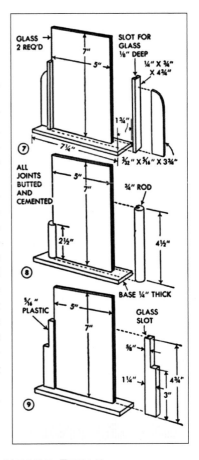

— STRIPED HEART BUILT

OF LAMINATED
PLASTIC SHEET —

When viewed from the front, this plastic heart shows a few fine vertical lines of color that widen into stripes as it is rotated slowly, and when viewed from the side the heart appears to be a solid color. The blank from which the heart is cut is built up of laminations of transparent thermoplastic cemented together. The plastic sheets may be of the same thickness, or of varying thicknesses from ¼ to ⅛ in. to provide different patterns. The plastic is first washed with acetone and then the surfaces to be joined are coated with colored fingernail polish. After the polish has dried, it should be sanded with No. 400 wet-or-dry sandpaper and wiped clean. When building up the laminations, use glacial acetic acid for a binder, shown in *Fig. 1*, wiping off any air bubbles. Press the sheets together with the fingers when the surfaces become tacky, but do not use clamps because this will press the polish out from between

the sheets, leaving a weak color or no color at all. Allow the block to set for at least 24 hours and then cut lengthwise strips, as in *Fig. 2*, about ⅜ to ½ in. thick. Using a template with the shape of a heart, saw the rough, as in *Fig. 3*, and round with a file, shown in *Fig. 4*. If a few extra minutes are spent with the filing, it will save much sanding time. Final sanding is done with No. 320 emery cloth, shown in *Fig. 5*, followed by No. 400 wet-or-dry sandpaper. While any fine abrasive polish can be

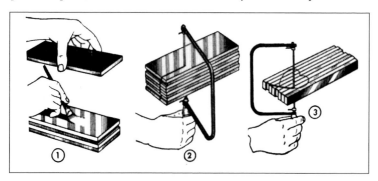

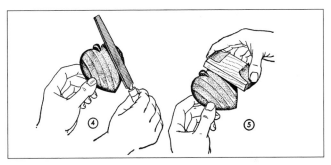

used, one made with a paste of tin oxide and water spread on a tightly stretched cloth works well. The heart is rubbed briskly over the cloth, rotating and turning it in the process. When the heart has the required polish, the hole for the chain is drilled with a No. 50 drill. This should be at an angle from both sides to avoid marring the polished surfaces. Polish the hole with a cotton string rubbed with abrasive.

— PICTURES "EMBROIDERED" IN WIRE —

Here's something new in wall pictures that are distinctively different and an incredibly easy and rewarding project for fathers and daughters to undertake. The pictures consist of bright wire attached to framed panels of fancy wood against which the wire picture casts a slight shadow to make it stand out boldly and produce a pleasing effect. All you need to make these unusual pictures are pliers, a small

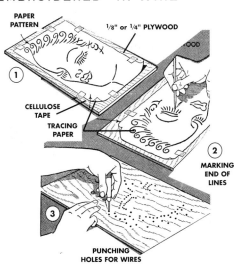

PAPER PATTERN

1/8" or 1/4" PLYWOOD

CELLULOSE TAPE

TRACING PAPER

MARKING END OF LINES

PUNCHING HOLES FOR WIRES

hammer, an awl, some old wire, and few pieces of thin wood. Magazines and newspapers provide an excellent source for suitable pictures to copy. Look for those made up mostly of outlines, such as the ones shown in *Fig. 5*. In tracing the picture, break up the lines into short lengths and avoid continuous lines. The wood should be selected to give the most pleasing contrast to the kind of wire used. Copper or enameled wire stands out nicely on light-colored woods, while brass or tinned wire looks best on darker woods. You can use fancy veneered plywood ⅛ to ¼ in. thick in walnut, mahogany or maple, or the top and bottom of a cigar box will do. The wood is first sanded smooth and finished by staining and waxing, or by leaving the wood natural and applying wax or linseed oil.

Center the tracing on the wood so that there will be about 1 in. or so of margin all around to allow for framing. Hold it in position with a few tabs of tape, as in *Fig. 1*. Now, with an awl or a sharply pointed nail, make a prick mark at the beginning and end of each line, as in *Fig. 2*. After this, remove the tracing and with the same tool, or with a small twist drill if the wood is ¼-in. thick, make a hole through the wood at each mark. The size of the hole is governed by the size of the wire used. A No. 22- or 20-gauge wire is about the right size. If the wire needs straightening, you can do so by drawing it over a dowel or other round surface. When all the holes are drilled, sand the front and back of the wood lightly to remove the rough edges.

From now on, it's just a matter of bending the wire to conform to the contour of each line of the pattern, which is done by laying it over the line to be copied and forming it with the fingers to correspond. At the ends of each line, the ends of the wire are bent downward with pliers to pass through the wood and extend about ¼ in. on the back. This procedure is followed until all the lines of the pattern are completed, after which the projecting ends are clinched, as shown in *Fig. 4*, by turning the picture face down on a soft-pine block and hammering the wire down in the direction of the grain.

— PLASTER CAST OF INFANT'S HAND —

Cast in plaster, an impression of a baby's hand or foot will be a wonderful keepsake for years to come. Use ordinary modeling clay that has been warmed until it is soft. Then place an embroidery hoop around it to form the side of the mold. Make an impression of the infant's hand or foot and pour a mixture of plaster of Paris into the mold. After the plaster has set, remove the hoop and lift the disk from the clay.

MODELING CLAY
HOOP   PLASTER

PULL (*or* PUSH) TOYS *for* TOTS

— THIS "WIGGLE TURK" AMUSES EVERYONE —

DIAGRAM FOR
LAYING OUT
THE "WIGGLE
TURK."

A handy girl can create an amazingly fun toy for little ones, with just a little help and supervision. Like a real turtle, as it moves its feet, tail, and head while it is pulled over the floor, the toy wood "turk" shown in the illustration will be particularly appealing to children. It is made of ½-in. wood obtainable almost anywhere, an empty thread

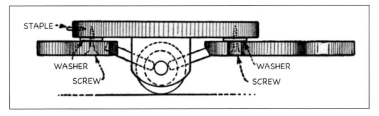

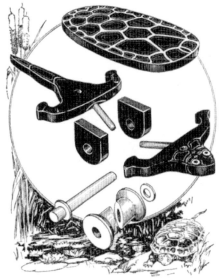

DETAILS OF THE TURTLE SHOWING ITS DURABLE CONSTRUCTION AND SIMPLE MECHANISM.

happens to be on hand, so that there will be a space of about ¼ in. between the parts of the spool. Washers are slipped on the shaft, and it is then put in the bearings, which are made of ½ in. wood that's cut to the shape shown in the detail drawing. The bearings are nailed to the back with a few small finishing nails. Holes are drilled and countersunk

spool of medium size, and a few short lengths of ⅛- or 3/16-in. dowel rod. The head and front legs are one piece, as are the tail and hind legs. The activating mechanism is a thread spool, sawed in two pieces with a diagonal cut. Both pieces are driven on a short length of dowel rod, or any small wooden rod that

through the center of the front and hind members as indicated and a hole is drilled diagonally in each member for a short piece of dowel rod, which is cut long enough to project into the slot in the spool without binding. Then the front and hind members are screwed loosely to the underside of the body with flat-head screws, washers being provided between these members and body to reduce friction.

To achieve the same shape and design as that shown in the drawing, cut a piece of paper 6 by 12 in. and lay off lines to make 1-in. squares. Then proceed to reproduce the outline, drawing the curves through the same sections of the squares. It is, of course, necessary to do the cutting with a fret saw or jigsaw. A fret saw can be purchased cheaply at almost any hardware store and will be found useful for many other purposes besides cutting out toys. After the parts are cut out—with care being taken to have the grain of the wood run lengthwise through the narrow sections such as the tail— dress down the rough edges with a smooth half-round file. Sandpaper is used to give the parts a smooth surface, and if you want to give the

toy an exceptionally good finish, apply a coat of shellac.

The painting of the turtle is a factor that adds considerably to its appearance. Quick-drying lacquers, which can be obtained in most paint or hardware stores, are very adaptable to toys of this kind. Keep in mind that bright contrasting colors are most appealing to the children, and proceed to paint the likeness of a real turtle. After the painting has been completed and is dry, drive a small staple or tack into the edge of the body just over the head and attach a string by which the toy can be pulled over the floor. When this is done the spool is revolved and a side-to-side movement given to the front and hind members, which will make the turtle appear to be walking naturally. The faster the turtle is pulled, the faster it will wiggle, until it seems to make a super-turtle speed.

— TOY DONKEY NODS AND WAGS ITS TAIL —

The most popular toys are those that move in imitation of some well-known object, and the donkey shown in the drawing is a good example of these. This engaging creature nods his head and wags his tail as he moves along. The outline is drawn on a ¾-in. block and sawed out with a scroll, band, or coping saw, and the head is sawed off, as indicated. A slot is then sawed up through the legs and part way into the body. A similar, but narrower, slot is cut in the back of the head. A strip of tin is used to connect the head to the body, as shown. A piece of tin, cut to the shape of a tail, is similarly attached in the slot behind. Both the tail and the tin strip that connects the head to the body are pivoted to the latter with small brads. Motion to the head and tail is imparted by wires that connect the parts to a screw eye underneath the wheeled base on which the figure is mounted. Flat strips of wood with rounded edges, which are attached to the revolving axles, strike the wires as the toy is pulled across a table, causing both head and tail to move up and down. The animal may be decorated as desired.

A TOY DONKEY THAT WAGS ITS TAIL AND NODS ITS HEAD WHEN DRAWN ACROSS A TABLE, HAS A SIMPLE MECHANISM THAT MAKES IT EASY TO CONSTRUCT.

— EASTER BUNNY PULL TOY —

A gaily colored bunny atop a large egg makes this wheeled toy attractive to the children. The egg and bunny are jigsawed in one piece from ¾-in. stock. After this, the legs are glued and nailed in place with brads, as overlays. Filler blocks 1½ in. wide are sawed to the same curvature as that of the lower part of the egg, and are nailed and glued to it. Side pieces of ¼-in. stock are nailed to the blocks. These have tabs projecting from the lower edges through which ¼-in. dowel axles are

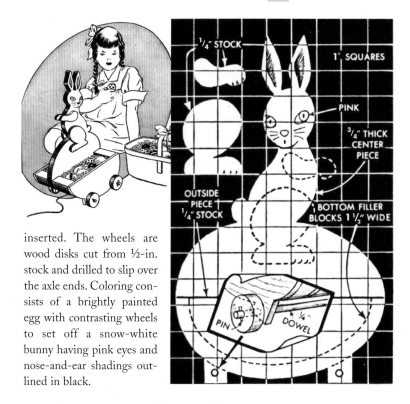

inserted. The wheels are wood disks cut from ½-in. stock and drilled to slip over the axle ends. Coloring consists of a brightly painted egg with contrasting wheels to set off a snow-white bunny having pink eyes and nose-and-ear shadings outlined in black.

BIG FUN

— ROCKING BIRDS AMUSE LITTLE TOTS —

These bird cutouts not only rock to amuse the kiddies, but are strong enough for them to sit on. The sides are screwed to wedge-shaped filler blocks that spread them so that the rocker will not tip over with its little rider. First, copy the outlines of the sides to ¼-in. plywood, hard-pressed board, or any other suitable material, and jigsaw them to shape. Then, form a length of 2-by-4-in. stock, cut the blocks as

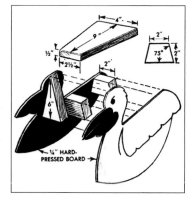

shown in the detail, and screw them in place. Fit the sides to them so that the top edge of the heads meet and the tails spread out. Screw a tapered saddle over the blocks, and you are ready to add the finishing touches. Sand the birds thoroughly to remove any rough spots or slivers that may injure the rider, then paint the work as indicated in the cross-hatched drawing. For clearest coloring, first apply a flat-white primer coat. When painting toys such as these, which require several different colors, it is best to use tube oil paints and a can of white enamel. Then any desired color may be mixed in small quantities without waste. If the birds are to be used outdoors, coat them with spar varnish.

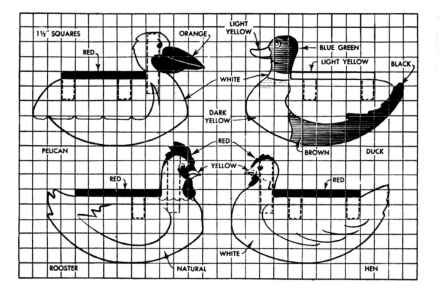

— IT'S FUN TO ROCK
BETWEEN THESE TWO BUNNIES —

Guarded on both sides by colorful cutouts of Peter Rabbit, this bunny rocker chair is sawed from ⅜-in. plywood and consists of four parts—a seat, back, and two sides. The rockers are integral with the sides. In assembling the chair, the edges of the seat and back are butted against the sides and fastened with glue and screws spaced about 3 in.

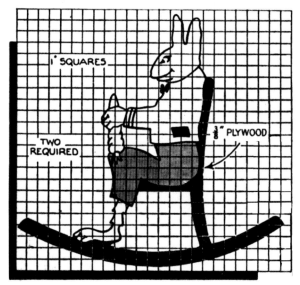

1" SQUARES

TWO REQUIRED

⅜" PLYWOOD

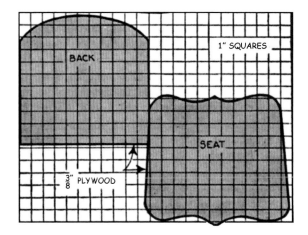

apart. Or, you can use cleats under the seat and behind the back for additional rigidity. The cleats are first screwed to the side, then the seat and back are screwed to the cleats. Painting in bright colors enhances the appearance. First, give the wood a coat of shellac and sand lightly when dry. Then finish as desired, painting the cutouts in identical colors on both sides. The original chair had dark-blue rockers, seat and back, and the bunny cutouts wore brown trousers and green jackets. Their faces, feet, and hands were pale pink. Black neckties, jacket pockets, and trouser stripes offer just the right contrast. The carrots in their hands are orange and the eyes are black with yellow pupils.

— A Black-Cat Bench for Children —

Children are always interested in bits of furniture that incorporate animal designs. One craftsman's children had a number of pet cats, so he was determined to construct a small settee or bench based upon a cat design. After some searching, he found a design that, with a little alteration, would serve very well for this purpose. The drawing shows one end piece of the settee drawn to scale. Because the craftsman's children were quite small, the scale he used was 1 in. for each division of the scale. It is very easy to enlarge this design to any desired dimensions. The tails of the cats support the back, so it is evident that the end pieces should be cut with the grain of the wood vertical. Also, a fairly close-grained hardwood should be used. The end pieces were cut from ⅝-in. material, a common fret saw being used for the purpose. A piece for the back was cut from 5/8-in. material, 14 by 24 in. in size. The seat measures 8 by 24 in., and was cut from ⅞ in. stock. These were inserted as shown by the dotted lines in the drawing. It will be noticed that the front of the seat is higher than the back and that the angle between the two is somewhat greater than 90 degrees. Because the feet of the bench were cut across the grain, they were reinforced with two pieces, 1½ in. square, nailed to the inside. To pre-

DESIGN OF THE ENDS OF THE BLACK-CAT BENCH

vent splitting, the holes for the nails were drilled before nailing.

When all the material was ready for assembly, the back had no padding. A piece of green-colored decorative burlap was fastened to the top edge of the back piece, the edges being turned under to make a smooth edge. This edge was fastened with small carpet tacks. The burlap was then stretched tight and tacked along both sides, but not turned over the edges. Finally, the bottom was turned and tacked to the narrow edge of the back. Then,

THE COMPLETED BENCH

as a finish, gimp was nailed over all edges, using upholstering nails for this purpose.

The seat was next upholstered. Burlap was tacked to the bottom about 1 in. from the edge, and gimp applied to provide a smooth edge. Next the ends of the burlap were drawn over the ends of the seat and fastened in like manner. The burlap was drawn firm but not stretched. When the three sides were fastened, curled hair was packed into the sack until it was about 1½ in. thick in the center, thinning out to all edges. Finally, the back was drawn under and tacked to the bottom. The seat was then turned over and beaten with a lath until all lumps had disappeared and the hair was uniformly distributed.

In assembling, the back is inserted first and nailed into place. Nails were used throughout so that they could be countersunk and puttied over. When the back had been placed, the seat was inserted so that the bottom edges of the back and the seat were flush. Then the seat was nailed in place.

In finishing, the settee was given a coat of ordinary black paint followed by two coats of gloss-black enamel. When this was thoroughly dry, the eyes, mouths, and whiskers were painted in white decorative enamel. An irregular band of white enamel was drawn just under the feet to separate them from the base proper. This settee has proved very popular with kiddies, and they prefer it to any of their other chairs or seats.

Materials

2 pieces, 22 by 12 by ⅝ in., for the ends

1 piece, 24 by 14 ⅝ in., for the back

1 piece, 24 by 8 by ⅞ in., for the seat

2 pieces, 12 by 1½ by 1½ in., for base reinforcement

Burlap, hair, paint, enamel, etc.

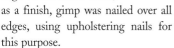

— Circus Elephants Give Child a Ringside Seat —

Your small child will take pride in possessing this gaily colored chair. Anyone can make it with a scroll saw and a screwdriver. All parts are cut from ½-in. plywood and assembled with flat-head screws. These should be countersunk carefully and puttied over. The chair looks nice with the elephants finished in light gray and the blankets painted on with a darker gray and bordered with brilliant orange.

— Utility Wagon for Toys —

Suitable as a sight-seeing bus for dolly, or as a moving van for toys, this all-purpose wagon is made from a few pieces of scrap wood and four skate wheels. Bottom and end pieces are cut from ½-in. stock and sides are strips of molding, which can be plain or shaped. Wheels are attached by bolts to short lengths of flat iron drilled and

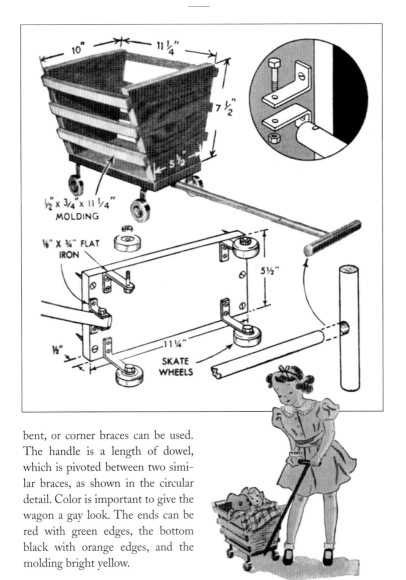

bent, or corner braces can be used. The handle is a length of dowel, which is pivoted between two similar braces, as shown in the circular detail. Color is important to give the wagon a gay look. The ends can be red with green edges, the bottom black with orange edges, and the molding bright yellow.

— PONY SLEIGH —

Any small child will be happy riding between these prancing ponies that are "harnessed" with jingling sleigh bells. A feature of the sleigh is that the seat is high enough so a child can be lifted in or out without having to bend over.

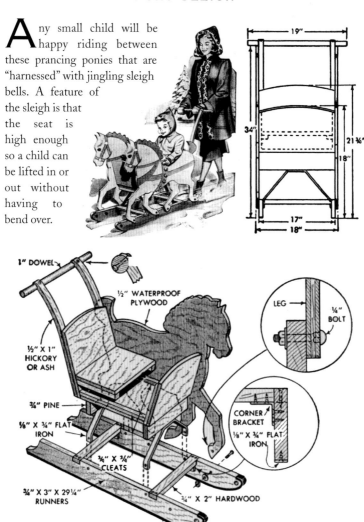

1" DOWEL

½" WATERPROOF PLYWOOD

½" X 1" HICKORY OR ASH

¾" PINE

⅛" X ¾" FLAT IRON

¾" X ¾" CLEATS

¾" X 3" X 29¼" RUNNERS

¾" X 2" HARDWOOD

LEG

¼" BOLT

CORNER BRACKET

⅛" X ¾" FLAT IRON

19"

34"

21⅜"

18"

17"

18"

Method of assembly, dimensions and materials are given in the detail and the pattern for sawing the ponies is shown on the crosshatched drawing. The hickory or ash handles are steamed and bent to shape. Finish the sleigh in bright colors.

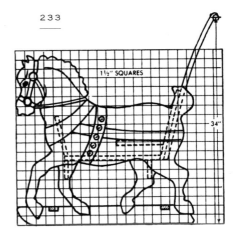

1½″ SQUARES

34″

— CATTLE TRAIN IN THE NURSERY —

Just to show that this is a cattle train, the animals extend their necks and wag their heads as the young engineer pilots the locomotive around the playroom. The car and engine are cut to the shape shown in the cross-hatched pattern. The front-axle support is pivoted on a nail, washers being inserted, as shown. It is turned for steering by lengths of ½-in. dowel that extend to a handlebar pivoted on a center pin, which is a short length of ½-in. dowel. Wheels of 1-in. stock are drilled for nails that are driven into the axle supports to serve as axles, washers being used here, too. The

cattle heads are glued to 2-in. lengths of ¼-in. dowel inserted loosely through holes drilled in the car to permit them to swing.

— ❖ ❖ ❖ —

THE BOY MECHANIC SERIES

— A NOTE FROM THE EDITORS —

If you've enjoyed *The Girl Mechanic*, you might like our *Boy Mechanic* books, our line of vintage titles from Popular Mechanics. To find a complete description of these books, please visit us at www.sterlingpublishing.com and type in Popular Mechanics, Girl Mechanic, or Boy Mechanic in the search field. They are available wherever books are sold.

We'd love to hear what you think about our books.
Please contact us directly with any queries and comments
by emailing our reader hotline, booklover@hearst.com.
We look forward to hearing from you.

INDEX